Business Invention

Business Needs You Not Investment

DR. SRIRAM ANANTHAN

© Copyright 2019 – Dr. Sriram Ananthan.

All rights reserved.

The contents of this book may not be reproduced, duplicated or transmitted without direct written permission from the author.

Under no circumstances will any legal responsibility or blame be held against the publisher for any reparation, damages, or monetary loss due to the information herein, either directly or indirectly.

Legal Notice:

This book is copyright protected. This is only for personal use. You cannot amend, distribute, sell, use, quote or paraphrase any part of the content within this book without the consent of the author.

CONTENTS

INTRODUCTION 1
WHY BUSINESS...5
   A. Save Tax..7
   B. Be your own boss 8
WHAT BUSINESS?..15
SET A GOAL...20
GAIN KNOWLEDGE IN THAT FIELD 27
STAY FOCUS..30
LESS INVESTMENT..37
BUSINESS ROADMAP 49
   1. Create the Company Name 50
   2.   Create a company logo..52
   3. Select a product or service 53
   4. Mission and vision 54
   5. Investment size and why you need this money, where you want to invest 55
   6. Study on competitors 60
   7. Plan marketing strategy: 61
   8. Business Projection:...66
   9. SWOT analysis..69
   10.   Franchise model 71
COLLECT DATA..79
YOUTUBE CHANNEL 86
   The Benefits of Using YouTube for Business 87

Types of videos for your YouTube business channel 92
Choose the right content for your channel 95
BUSINESS IDEA 97
    A. INVESTMENT ADVISER: 98
    B. HOUSE INSPECTOR 100
    C. INSURANCE BROKER 102
    D. MORTGAGE BROKERS 106
    E. PLUMBING COMPANY 107
    F. ELECTRICIAN COMPANY 111
    G. PAINTING 114
    H. HOME FOOD 117
    I. CLEANING COMPANY 119
    J. Book Keeping Consultation: 122
    K. BUSINESS CONSULTANT: 126

INTRODUCTION

Enterprise invention is a process of organizing innovative notions, workflows, methods, amenities, or yields. As with the information technology invention, where technologies need to be deployed in innovative means to generate a supplementary well-organized plus swift association, the invention of corporate must permit the accomplishment of objectives all over the association, whereas accomplishing central corporate objectives and ingenuities in the business must outlook in the forefront. Revolution repeatedly twitches with indication cohort, which borders notions in suggesting conferences. Subsequently, officials inspect the lucrativeness, possibility and allure of every notion. Discoveries of corporations must increase prevailing products, amenities or procedures, or it must resolve a problem; or it must influence new patrons.

Current specimens of corporate developments comprise the primer of the Dyson vacuum cleaner, whose originator and namesake James Dyson proclaimed in announcements that he desired to ripen an improved product by smearing industrialized cyclone machineries to home-based machines. Ride-sharing corporations (Zipcar, Uber and Lyft) are an illustration of a provision novelty. Gillette has owed its Mach3 razors for ground-breaking expertise.

Why business inventions are important?

The persistence of the discovery course is to generate an innovative worth for the association. This assessment may be able to consequence from making new income openings or snowballing income over current frequencies. After generating competence that protects time, money or mutually booth; or enhancements in throughput or enactment.

In a squat, revolution must tip to greater revenues.

In tally, the outcomes of the discovery method of a corporation would fetch an inexpensive improvement. It is premeditated to support the association cultivate and attain or smooth outstrip tactical objectives.

Invention vs. Innovation

Invention and innovation are thoroughly connected; nonetheless, the two notions are not identical. An invention is an entirely original formation. The procedure of corporate revolution might yield an origination; nonetheless, the tenure is wider and comprises the submission of a prevailing notion or rehearsal in an innovative method or the submission of fresh technology to prevailing merchandise or procedure to recover it. To comprehend the alteration, deliberate the succeeding: The telephone is an origination, but the smartphone is a development.

Business Innovation Cycle

Although here is no amalgamated plan for enterprise modernization, corporations that are unswervingly efficacious in enterprise modernization partake a repeatable course to engender, check, and progress notions may be able to tip to modernization.

The succession is frequently alienated into four portions. It flinches with the construction of concepts in key zones (business mockups, advertising, procedures, products and facilities). The succession drives through the detection and then transfers on to expansion and conveyance.

The first stage emphases on the formation and recording of philosophies as well as the introductory calculation of whether these philosophies can produce worth.

The next phase focuses on testing the ideas through pilot programs or proofs of concepts, in which ideas and their value are further valued.

The latter two stages are around mounting ideas, shifting them into manufacture and assimilating them into usual business actions.

Business front-runners frequently use dissimilar terms for every of these stages. For instance, several mentions to the first stage documentation and the last stage execution, but the ladders for every stage are fundamentally similar.

Some administrators and executive's disrupt the series down into even extra stages, unravelling rudiments such as investigation, challenging, and appraisal as discrete ladders.

Models of the invention

Business developments can be alienated into diverse classes or prototypes.

Several are easy to understand, such as invention or procedure development. Extra sorts and whatever they mean are:

- Business Modeling: Evolving and executing fresh, exclusive perceptions that upkeep the economic practicability of business, counting its undertaking.
- Modeling an industrial model: generating an innovative diligence or stirring a society into a different diligence.
- Revenue Model Invention: Enhancements and / or vicissitudes to an administration's income cohort agenda, an objective also abridged as a business model novelty.

Revolutionary against evolutionary

Business developments can correspondingly be categorized as revolutionary or evolutionary.

Revolutionary business creations tip to radical vicissitudes to merchandises, amenities, procedures, etc. that frequently abolish or substitute a prevailing business model.

Evolutionary inventions comprise slighter, further unremitting perfections that are imperative but not melodramatically ample to turn a business or a market into a new prototype.

Unsettling invention is a class that highpoints the disparaging feature of the revolutionary invention; this term denotes to corporation developments that upshot in the development of a first-hand market that relocates a prevailing or alike considerable alteration in a class of merchandises or amenities.

Business Invention

WHY BUSINESS

Business Invention

Beginning a business can be frightening. Magnates who stand lucky enough to twitch effective minor businesses are considering for immense plunders - welfares that you miscue if you keep on as a salary recipient for the cessation of your lifecycle. Though solitary you can choose for yourself if you are prepared to leave your occupation and dive into your individual business, at this juncture are certain plunders to go unaccompanied:

- Freedom and litheness. You have supplementary liberty and independence for you. As soon as your business is steadfastly recognized, you undoubtedly have the suppleness to make certain you do not miscue the instants and proceedings that matter utmost to you.
- Individual serenity. Possessing and running your individual business can be further sustaining and satisfying than functioning for somebody besides. Many prosperous minor business proprietors escalate that they relish the admiration they merit from their contemporaries since they partake the nerve to go out on their own.
- Power. Do not be astonished if supremacy is one of your aims. If it's your business, you can permit your workers to do it the mode you need. When power matters to you, reflect about in what way to use it beneficially.
- Money The danger of not devouring a consistent wage appraisal can pay off if you possess your personal business. You can get opulent in a minor business or at tiniest make it economically very decent. Though most businesspersons do not get opulent, some do.

In datum, several people do business since they need to study new abilities. It's a self-motivated way to enlarge your knowledge.

These are just a limited number of the abilities that are indispensable to many recent businesspersons. For every element, I've allied a guide to support you absorb the ability:

- Search Engine Optimization (SEO)
- Online Marketing / Growth Hacking
- Copywriting
- Social media
- Business planning

A. Save Tax

This is clearly not the foremost motive for beginning a business, but it benefits. As a minor business possessor, you can be capable to acquire tax pauses that will benefit your business - and even tax disruptions that eventually aid you as entities.

As I live in the US (and the profligate accessible online appraisals are engrossed on the US), I will make emphasis on whatever Americans can get after interpretation of their taxes on beginning a business. Here is the first part of the extensively prevalent IRS itself:

"Business costs are the costs of exercising a trade or business. These expenses are usually deductible if the business is operated profitably."

Conferring to the Houston Chronicle, this means that you might be able to remove donations such as publication contributions, telephone amenities, tourism miles, and involvement of specialized connotations. Heck, if you work in a home office, you may be capable of subtracting a percentage of your rent payment from the taxes. If you need somewhat to route your business, this can tip to a presumption.

The IRS also aids decrease the danger to American businesspersons. Conferring to Mashable, you can write off losses from your business, which means that a side business can upkeep your tax reappearance.

In his blog, Steven Chou premeditated that a regular American can get a 10% write-off complete a pact.

Tax commandments differ from country to country (surprise!), Therefore discover how your country knobs business taxes (here's some startup statistics for Australia and the UK).

B. Be your own boss

Initiate your personal business by the approach, is one of the utmost influential conducts to switch your life and receive further money month after month.

You can twitch with just a few hours a week - even if you devour a job. And greatest of all, you pick your instructions, select schemes that concern you, and encounter fascinating people.

And the start is not tough. You do not want an LLC, an elegant store, or an operative. You only want an accurate organization.

Step 1: Find a business idea

This is perhaps the greatest unnerving zone for humans. In datum, the most mutual purpose people did not twitch a business parenthetically is the point that they "do not partake a decent business idea."

Though, this is just a cerebral fence - one that you can effortlessly overawe by observing at a zone: your strong point.

At this juncture are four enquiries you can enquire to catch a firm business idea:

1. What skills do you have?

Whatever do you recognize and do you recognize well? These are the abilities and information that you partake learned.

Reflect of it inversely: we wage all the time for adept awareness (eg language schoolings, university progressions, instrument training). Predict what? You can likewise be this tutor.

Instances: language talents in an overseas language, encoding services, cooking services, etc.

2. What do your friends say that you are great?

I adore this query. It cannot solitary be a fine little character enhancement, but it can also be unbelievably skimpy.

Transcribe to your family and friends on Facebook or enquire them. IRL: What can I do well? Your responses can be altered into side business notions.

Examples: teaching habits, relationship guidance, style sense, etc.

3. What are you doing on a Saturday morning?

What are you undertaking on a Saturday morning, afore everybody else is up? This can be amazingly informative, on behalf of which you are zealous and for what you like to devote time.

I devour an acquaintance who dears clothes. Your Saturday morning comprises of sense fashion blogs and keeping a Pinterest account occupied with clothing and design concepts.

I catch the subsequent fascinating: she not ever believed of spiraling it into a business. It's somewhat she adores to do, but I pledge that there are a percentage of people forfeiting $ 500 for a Skype-style conference that might be done from the ease of their private home. Certain people even wage her thousands for her own client.

Examples: cruising fashion websites, functioning on your car, interpreting fitness subreddits, etc.

4. What do you already pay for?

You do not even partake to piece for your powers and aptitudes. In its place, you can gaze for things that you previously paid for.

After all, we wage people to do numerous diverse things. There is no aim why you can't go one of these things into your personal online business.

Examples: Unsoiled your home, verve with your pet, cook mealtimes, etc.

Find at smallest amount 3 - 5 answers to each of these queries. In conclusion, you have 12 - 20 business notions that you can twitch by the way.

First choose one of these thoughts and endure with stage two. Do not concern, if you do not texture it. Well ahead, you can permanently return to your tilt and choose extra one. That's the loveliness of this scheme.

Step 2: Find top paying customers

Ruling consumers do not partake to be a nightmarish for emotionless calling / e-mailing. All you devour to do is recollect that the enormous bulk of your rivalry is absolutely awful.

They are so horrifying that you will promptly share with 99.999% of others if you put slight energy into their unique spread. This is particularly factual for job panels like Craigslist.

Yes, this Craigslist. In a statement, this is one of the finest seats to make leads as an outworker.

This is as probable consumers, and customers who change to places in quest of freelancers do not get the finest applicants. In its place, they acquire people to mass-shoot the boilerplate emails (if any), eager to mark an entrance.

You will not do that, however. In its place, you'll want a certain time to use the email in stage 3 to generate a flawless arena for your amenities.

This does not just smear to Craigslist - you can practice this in any workplace. The significant is to be slightly improved than the normal and eager to check rare dissimilar emails.

Step 3: Place your work (with scripts!)

To grasp prospective consumers and customers, you want to be approachable to their desires.

It is undeveloped human psychology. Envisage, you are on the first day and everybody new can dialog about what they want and their needs. You will snitch out of the restroom window inside minutes.

But envisage that they would enquire interrogations about you and actually appeared absorbed in your life and glitches. You would be considerably more attentive in a second date, correct?

The similar fact smears when you expect a customer. You want to toil out your original influence rendering to your wants and anxieties.

Organism a geek, I've settled a 5-line email pattern that lets you refer to the flawless email arena. It covers:

1. Overview. You need to construct a camaraderie by presenting yourself and how you discern the client.
2. The bid. Dialog about them. What do you need to do on behalf of her? Why are you decent for this part? They want

to do investigation in the association to find out what they want assistance with.
3. Benefits. Study how your effort is advantageous to your trade. Are you going to devote supplementary time for her? Do you want to make the most of your revenue by the X amount?
4. The base in the entrance. This is a definitive method that performs an ancient psychological hoax to get the customer to decide to a small contract so you can request for a better arrangement later.
5. The call to achievement. Be unblemished and request them if they need to endure. The request to achievement is a dangerous portion of this lettering.

Step 4: Vote for the perfect price

The amounts are perplexing for every novice. And it's filled with queries like, "Is $XX / hour too abundant? Is it too diminutive? "Or" Had better I charge per hour or afterwards scheme? "

There are no secure guidelines for tariffs - but here are limited convenient directions of thumb to aid you to catch the one that outfits you finest:

1. Take three-zero procedure

Just yield your superlative income, leave three zeros, and before you know it, you have your hourly amount!

For instance, presume you indeed want to receive a smallest amount $ 40,000. Just yield out the three zeros from the conclusion, and you currently take your rate: 40 USD / hour.

2. Double your "grudge number"

Business Invention

I adore this as it is together actually thought-provoking and operative. Ask yourself: What is the nethermost rate you will effort for, which irritates you afterwards your work?

For instance, assume you are employed for $ 15 an hour at VERLE LEAST. Just twofold that number so you can currently make $ 30 an hour.

3. Do what the next guy is doing

This technique is extremely modest: Go to Google and guise for the regular hourly proportion for the facility you bid. You will partake a decent sense of where to flinch when you load your clients.

Just choose one of the approaches overhead and practice it as the preliminary price. As soon as you twitch heaping your customers, you have a decent impression if it is adequate for you.

Afterwards your first clients you can "regulate" your prices. Did you make $ 30 / hour? Start by charging $ 40 or even $ 50. Once more, there are no immovable rules on how abundant you must charge. Just twitch tweaking till you find an amount that you are pleased with.

Step 5: Invest in yourself

Your aims will alter as quickly as you distinguish how to twitch a business. You may need to be paid more money just to upsurge your revenue. You may need to measure so you can consent your job and emphasis on your work. The best way to do that is to capitalize on yourself.

One thing that ensues very often to people who have not occupied the time to capitalize on themselves and practice how these stuff works is that they produce so-called generalization stages.

A complete additional speculation in this one is to study how the thoughts halt down cerebral fences to stop you from attaining your goals. I would like to discourse some of the greatest significant reasons for beginning a business.

Business Invention

WHAT BUSINESS?

Business Invention

What kind of business should you start?

Grounded on the understandings of businesspersons who are effectively certain what kind of business to flinch, we inquire six crucial interrogations that you ought to ask yourself in instruction to conclude the flawless business idea that you can reply to. To answer the eventual question of whatever kind of business you must twitch with, you must first deliberate these queries. With these six answers, grounded on your discrete aims and understandings, you can trace the unsurpassed firm you need to twitch:

1. What experience do I have?

Ashley Hill, originator and CEO of College Prep Ready, utters she started her business since she had individual achievement bankrolling her college fantasy.

"I've been observing for the encounters that students and families facade when forfeiting for college, to aid improve my essential message and amenities," she says.

From her involvement and investigation, she erudite that there was a market for the information she had to bid. With the Americans, who had tons of dollars in loans for loaning to students, Hill unwritten the discomfort points of students and parents as they moved in the college application and the process of financial assistance? She accepted that understanding and transformed herself into a business that alleviated the problems she had understood.

Likewise, Victoria Garlick, CEO of Occasion Amenities matchmaking website Air Events Global, trusts that they select a business founded on involvement and abilities. She's erected on a 20-year profession in occasion development.

"When determining what kind of business to twitch, I observed at my private and specialized antiquity and what I might do as occasion manager," says Garlick.

2. What do I do with passion?

An additional mutual reference that businesspersons part with us is to find and follow their desire. Nick Ehret, the creator of Varieteas, has a desire for tea. So he constructed a fruitful business by curating field teas for his monthly donation boxes.

He is a first-rate tea devotee who recognized he might get his desire into a business. His guidance to people in selecting a business is "to select somewhat that you are tremendously ardent about because you will effort with it all day and every day."

Brian Davis, CEO of Spark Rental, pledges to a Japanese idea called ikigai. It means "reason to be". In this situation, rendering to Davis, a certainly decent business idea is the border among four things: what you compelled to do, what you can do well, what you can be salaried for and what that world desires.

3. What problem can I solve?

We all distinguish that requirement is the mother of discovery, but smearing that information to the business biosphere was not continuously the following step. A businessperson who changes this essential into a business plan could quickly develop a productive businessperson. As every customer can express you, there are glitches and agony points in nearly every manufacturing. Ruling out what these problems and disorganizations are - and emerging a business strategy to address these subjects - is an unquestionable method to find the correct business track.

Take, for instance, the dog bed business Big Barker. This business made $ 4.75 million in income in 2016. Eric Shannon, Creator and CEO, saw an obvious problem in the dog bed market. "I started Big Barker since there was a big unruly big dog proprietors had to contract with. They had to alter their dog beds once or twice a year since they were not decent enough to transmit the weight of a big dog."

Shannon requests promising businesspersons to resolve big problems: "The superior the problem you resolve, the better the prospects of your business."

4. What is my lifestyle attitude?

Your business objective can be millions of dollars in income and thousands of workers - and that's acceptable. Possibly the supreme significant thing for you is selecting a business prototypical that wires your perfect work-life equilibrium.

Antonella Pisani was vice president of worldwide e-commerce for Fossil and has detained management locations with JCPenney, Guitar Center and ProFlowers. Her key attention, however, was roving and captivating images. Meaning that she would prefer the flexibility to follow those benefits, Pisani discerned she needed a supple business model that wanted neither space nor portfolio.

This was the motivation for the conception of their websites, the authorized voucher code and the FACT Properties. These supple, web-based businesses have permitted her to toil from Antarctica, the Arctic, Bhutan, Morocco and other republics.

5. How much capital do I have available?

The thin startup was not a craze. In fact, the idea rose from an unavoidable and lasting fact about opening a business - people do not want to danger their life investments for a business idea that they do not until now have to demonstrate or make lucrative.

A good instance of this is Robert Lomax, who with RSL Educational, founded a teaching corporation geared to the requirements he saw as an educator in his specialized life. Obligations to his schooling involvement, he not only documented holes in the textbook market but also specified the occasion to retain his job and progress new merchandises. Ever since Lomax had a constant profit in establishing his company, he was gifted to evade debt and minimalize danger as his company produced.

And he would not have completed it any otherwise. Bestowing to Lomax, his method is perfect since it allows you to "take your time and discover your philosophies correctly."

6. Which ideas can I simply test?

Facebook CEO Mark Zuckerberg once said, "Transport rapidly breakdown things. If you do not break whatever, do not transport fast enough. "

In other verses, your business idea must be somewhat that you can demonstrate (or disprove) initially. If you do not have understanding in the merchandise advancing industry, vexing out a logistics company would be expensive. As an alternative, ponder about the deeper-hanging fruits in trades that concern you.

Marc Roche, the co-founder of Annuities HQ, a Canadian online reserve for superannuation merchandises, proposes investigating with family and friends in progress to last penetrating the Internet.

"Do not be frightened to try a small number of ideas before selecting a way," says Roche. "Get some rudimentary investigation online and get a logic of which impression is value the time and exertion to develop a corporation."

SET A GOAL

If you actually need to donate to the achievement of your business, you necessarily need to define your business objectives, particularly afore you twitch. For some people, the aim is the liberty to do whatever they want, at whatever time they want, without anybody effective them or else. For others, the economic sanctuary is the objective.

Background objectives is an indispensable portion of selecting the correct company for you. If your business does not encounter your private objectives, you may not be happy to wake up each morning and attempt to brand the business a victory. As soon or later, you will stop troubling the notion to work.

In the modest circumstance, an aim is just somewhat you aim for. Nevertheless, goals subsidize knowingly to prosperous business progress in numerous ways. In the commencement, the procedure powers you to set objectives, reflect about what you suppose from your business, and how development can or may not prosper. This procedure helps to propose directions for attaining this growth, which can importantly improve your probabilities of attaining your aims at all.

Reason of the Goal Setting:

Businesspersons must not be frightened of setting marks or estimates, as this is not a drawback at all. It is also significant to distinguish that goal setting is not just about income. This may narrate to origination, employee retention, service contributions, or whatsoever that is imperative to cultivating your business. There are four explanations why you must set objectives for your association:

1. Measure success

Decent administrations must continuously stab to recover, produce and become more lucrative. Goal setting is the strongest way to amount the company's achievement. If you aspect at your business for three or five years, you are beholding yonder the strategic side of your business, observing in its place for a much further macroeconomic opinion that lets you look at the business from an economical, business, or business viewpoint.

2. Cohesion of the leadership team

Setting objectives safeguards that everybody distinguishes what the leading is and what it all of it on. If your management squad obviously comprehends what you are vexing to attain, it will deliver an enhanced explanation for the selections you may make concerning signing, gaining, inducements, sales agendas, or other economic choices. This eliminates much of the doubt related to not sympathetic commercial goals.

3. Knowledge is power

As soon as your aims are distinct, you can progress a cavernous indulgent of the influence of strategic conclusions and occupy yourself with planned goals. For instance, if you have a financial plan that receipts income into account, you'll better comprehend the influence of a superior acquisition or a huge new client. I've protracted that evidence is supremacy and the more you know, the improved choices you can mark.

4. Review the mid-year goals

If you fixed aims prompt and unceasingly observe your business alongside these aims, you can change the progress mid-year or as desired. For example, suppose you have set your evolution object at 20 percent over the foregoing year, but throughout the second section, you discover that your economic predictions are not following as predictable. You can change your income and expenditure objectives to reproduce your business's tendencies. If you have not set objectives, this evidence is not so observable and conclusive achievement is more problematic.

Business Invention

It is tremendously significant to know that location business objectives for no association agreements triumph. Though, there is a portion to be alleged if you do not fly older the armchair of your pants. If you take the time to gaze at your business from a comprehensive viewpoint, you will setback more assurance in the forthcoming and how your business can enhance it. We cannot forecast the future, but we can surely strategize it.

Aims also offer you a charter in which to work. This application your labors by serving you eradicate travels that do not help realize the objectives you set. A very significant part of this structure is a schedule. Every good goal has a schedule, and this timetable will overwhelmingly touch your movements. When scenery goals, pay courtesy to the following possessions:

- Specificity. You have an improved casual of accomplishing a specific goal. Assets hovering is not a detailed goal; to assemble $ 10,000 by July 1st.
- Optimism. Be optimistic when setting your aims. Being capable to wage the bills is not precisely a stimulating objective. Reaching economic safety spells out your objective in a more optimistic way, increasing your energy to accomplish it.
- Sanity. If you fixed an objective of making $ 100,000 a month, if you have not earned so ample in a year, that goal is impractical. Twitch with small paces, eg. By snowballing your monthly revenue by 25 percent. Once your first aim is accomplished, you can spread for better objectives.
- Short and long term. Short-term aims can be grasped within weeks to a year. Long-term aims can be five, ten or even 20 years. They must be meaningfully overhead the short-term goals, but still be accurate.

There are integers of features to deliberate when setting aims:

- Income. Many businesspersons do business to attain monetary refuge. Contemplate around how abundant money you want to accept in your first year of the procedure and each year up to five years later.
- Lifestyle. These comprise degrees such as travel, waged hours, reserves in private possessions and topographical location. Are you prepared to travel or move broadly? How many hours do you want to work? What assets are you ready to risk?
- Types of work. When setting objectives for the nature of work, you need to elect whether you want to work outside, in the office, with computers, on the phone, with numerous people, with children, and so on.
- I satisfy. Envisage: Numerous people go around business to gratify their personalities. Possessing a business can be very self-centered, particularly if your effort in a business is fashionable or thrilling. You must choose how significant the gratification of the personality is to you and which business finest encounters that requisite.

The supreme significant law of the objective is uprightness. As you open your eyes to your final goals, you can brand your conclusions more self-assured and more effective.

Advantages of the Goal Setting:

Aims are an imperative constituent to the accomplishment of any business, counting the business biosphere. Aims aid as a leader to save you on a path in problematic times and to avert you from being unfocussed by insignificant things. Aims also deliver welfares in extents such as preparation, enthusiasm, and attaining rapid outcomes.

Specify direction for a company

Aims can set an upcoming course for your business that ropes you and your workforces in day-to-day management. For instance, if you need to retain office expenditures to a smallest for the year, you can struggle the enticement of obtaining a compact office apparatus, if not essential. If you aim to produce your business, you can select to capitalize on the revenue you take by gaining a huge customer to generate an extra profession.

Facilitation of business planning

Aims aid you design your business. You can set the aim of aggregate sales by 25 percent in the impending year. Though, after additional deliberation, you understand that this is not conceivable assumed the present scope of your sales power. Part of your preparation may consequently comprise employing two new salespeople inside the next 60 days.

Motivate employees to perform

Conferring to the Allusion for Business website, aims can correspondingly be used as a motivational utensil for your workforces. If you need to upsurge sales, you can contrivance an enticement program that offers your salespeople a cash prize to meet exact goals. You can also inspire all workers if your business can diminish expenditure by a firm proportion.

Restrict stress and keep focus

Aims can aid decrease strain. Deprived of aims to guide you, you may cultivate the inclination to fence from one plan or duty to one more, relatively than converging on the crucial desires of your business. As an upshot, you may discover that your total production grieves and you will marvel what you are truly attaining, and you generate a sagacity of trepidation.

Less wasted time

When you set an aim, you must too generate a step-by-step strategy to attain that aim. This can aid you to achieve a chore quicker since there is a smaller amount propensity to stray from the passage. You devote less time on unimportant or unfertile events and take a straighter path to reaching the goal. For instance, if you need to upsurge the income of your current customer base, do not waste time considering different businesses.

GAIN KNOWLEDGE IN THAT FIELD

Business Invention

Whether you involve yourself in continually fantasizing of being your own superior or being driven by joblessness, underemployment or luckless occupation, beginning your personal business may be further appealing than ever. Nevertheless, corporate evasion charges are as frightening as our present unemployment rates.

I at all times say that if you do not formulate, be ready to fail. One technique to make these arrangements to overcome the probabilities of ensuing in your good turn is to increase industry understanding.

Here are 5 methods to increase this understanding (and in particular cases produce a little superfluous dollars) afore you get completely tangled in your fresh business.

Take a part-time job in your target industry: If you famine to open a restaurant charter and have not ever toiled in foodservice afore, you must cogitate a part-time restaurant occupation, such as an immediate and weekend occupation, afore parting your existing job or your job pursuit overdue it. This will aid you to judge whether you like the industry, whether it's a decent occasion, how you supposed it was, and whether it turns in well with your aptitudes and your nature. These are all significant things you must distinguish afore capitalizing your money in a different business.

Talk to your future customers: Clients are the major asset of your business. But respectable market exploration is problematic. Find on sale what desires and requirements your forthcoming customers have (and how accountable they are to pact with them) by captivating on a customer facility job in your mark industry. When you toil in customer facility, you can realize first-hand in what way your customers reflect, turn and expend!

Learn from someone who was there. Question: What do utmost people dialogue around most? Response: yourself businesspersons are no dissimilar. Ask businesspersons who have stood in the dugouts for years to understand if they can devote time in an evidence meeting to study about the drawbacks of the industry. Or even improved, see if you can gumshoe them for a day or two, or do a voluntary internship to study about a fruitful being (or "somebody"). If you can bargain and dialogue those who have not remained efficacious, it will permit for even more profound erudition. If you do not discern somebody who is suitable for the bill, ask your particular, proficient, and societal networks to get in trace with these business possessors.

Starting Jobbie: A jobbie is my term for a sideline that makes money (also recognized as a lateral business). With a job, you can check the viability of a company with a distinct budget afore you get tangled. If your industry comprises a creation rather than a facility, grow, build, and test archetypes to test the petition and purpose of the product in relation to your day job or job hunt. Both methods permit you to advance industry acquaintance, and if you twig to a budget, you will not be saving your life.

Change Career: As a substitute for a part-time job, take a full-time job in your objective industry. Find out if you can look like a company that desires to start the business you famine to start up, even if you want to take a few footsteps in your vocation. Not only are you learning the business from scrape, but it's a good trial to see if you can be encouraged. If you cannot go up in an alternative company's business and aspect a lot like the business you want to flinch, ponder again afore setting up your personal business.

STAY FOCUS

Business Invention

There are usually only three motives to twitch your personal business: First, you have a countless idea and famine to be your identifiable boss. Second, you sense you can do whatever you do well than everyone, particularly your boss. And three, you have. No matter by what means you do that, utmost of us twitch without adequate money, deprived of adequate people or time, and deprived of sufficient information to go our opinions into lucrative and flourishing businesses.

It's prodigious to daydream big, but your start-up wants a laser emphasis at first to seizure the consideration of the market and stockholders. Google has completed it with exploration engines, Apple with a PC and even Walmart by low values.

A business idea I've seen certain time before that syndicates the good topographies of numerous prevalent social networks on a site does not. If you try to do the whole thing at once, it perhaps means that none of the objects is operational correctly. Also, it's nearly impossible to inscribe a message that highpoints your proposal in the thoughts of customers. I cannot envisage a company that goes into the luminary with a comprehensive focus.

These are the sensible reasons why a laser emphasis clues to the company's preliminary achievement:

1. The time to market is critical.

It receipts too abundant time to shape procedures and products to use a comprehensive approach. In the meantime, small contestants will develop, seize your business occasions and steal your objective customers.

2. It is important to keep infrastructure costs low.

Every company needs basic gear and substructure as well as constant progress costs. The effort to appreciate the big vision at once worldwide costs a lot of money. Getting more money is hard, but not so hard, as building the big substructure and getting it right the first time.

3. You have to be nimble.

Every positive start-up I know had to escape, texture, or revolve rapidly to find out what their customers really want, and what really works in merchandise project and advertising. Tired harvests and the countless philosophy that bonds everything do not allow you to rapidly familiarize to marketplace changes and mistakes.

4. Innovation leads to market leadership.

Success needs market management in your creation part, and it's easy to see that concentrating on more crops and facilities diminishes your emphasis and attention. Market management is not a one-time thing, but incessant invention or you will gap behind.

5. Maintaining quality is the key.

The extra you attempt to work in equivalent, the stiffer it is to uphold quality. Reminisce the ancient saying that "you solitary have a gamble to make a good first imprint." Clients are indecisive, and good excellence and customer service are problematic even with an attentive product.

6. The personal bandwidth is limited.

When stuff gets too untidy and multifaceted, and you too are uncertain of urgencies, people become disenchanted, tired, lose inspiration, and incline to give up effortlessly. A laser focus is calmer to interconnect, calmer to accomplish, and more probable to run fast and fine.

Important Ways to Get Focused

But some way we get preceding these steeplechases and put our thoughts into act. Resolution is one thing, but concentrating on what totals in the short term is unconditionally significant. To make certain you're opening a steady, rising business, here are my topmost seven instructions to aid get your business off the earth:

1. Focus on profitable customers.

Captivating new customers is serious to a first-hand business, but it's even more significant to save those you've functioned rigid on. Eventually, your business will be lucrative, contingent on how many recurrent customers you have. Also, emphasis on customers who devote a lot. Too frequently new businesspersons search any business, rather than "perfect" customers and customers.

2. Focus on the cash flow.

The cash flow statements must be completed weekly and in the minutest new companies every day. Find out how much income you prerequisite to put on the bank each day to make a revenue from the twitch. Then you can really achieve your income and income budgets.

3. Focus on the productive time.

At the opening, you have to make at slightest 80 percent of your day in the money. Vending, advertising and distribution are where you brand money. In other verses, sitting behind a desk or counter is a murderer for startups.

4. Focus on what works and sells.

As a startup proprietor, it's easy to make emphasis on whatever that does not work. Though, you must actually pay courtesy to what the marketplace expresses you to work. Halt annoying to sell or do things the market does not need. Startups need to be actually supple in getting to what works and what makes the most money.

5. Focus on customer service.

Of course, you need the customers to arise back, but the utmost of all, you want optimistic word of entrance. Aid your customers well and make it calm for them to mention their friends to you. But retain in mind that decent service only works if you permit it on to persons who escalate it (see point 1).

6. Concentrate on hiring only the best team members.

Never relax for the finest of an evil cluster. Continuously look for somebody who is inordinate. It can charge you 10 to 20 percent extra, but these folks will be value the price by assisting you to construct a fruitful business.

7. Focus on quality, not quantity.

When initial, businesspersons often fall into the trap of "superior is better". Sometimes smaller amounts and higher superiority - and thus a complex price and a higher yield border - are better. The same smears to the number of your clienteles and staffs. I'd rather have 10 great patrons than 100 regulars.

8. Focus on Streamline tasks

Enhancing tasks help you emphasis on getting ongoing by not trailing time. An updated task is done in the meekest way. You can easily adjust any task by concentrating on the calmest route from opinion A to point B. You can use organization tools like Trello and Loose to keep you up to date. You can also improve your daily responsibilities by making sure that you are occupied on analogous tasks at the same time. Do you need to write a bulletin and blog access? Run them in quick sequence, so you do not have to adjustment between hat and thinking style.

The justification should also comprise the allocation of errands. There are only so many hours a day, and as a formation creator, you need to attention on the tasks that only you can do. If another person has the services to do what you are working on, it should be vicarious to them. By allotting tasks, you modernize your day and allow you to make emphasis on the most important supplies of your startup.

9. Focus on creating a to-do list

We need to volte-face the to-do list. Many people create their to-do lists with the outlook of a crusader who never gets tired, distracted or interrupted. This is not the day of an organizer. Build your to-do list so you can focus on key tasks you need to do first and bound yourself to three to five tasks. Keep in mind that only 50 percent of finalized tasks are done in a single day.

The tasks that are on the list and are not done are more likely never to be done. Make your to-do list every night before departing your desk and make sure you only have the tasks you know you can do the next day.

10. Do something for your business every day

No matter what day it is, do one article for your corporate. Take a step to completing a professional goal, whether it's a holiday, your birthday, or just a Saturday. If you do by slightest one thing for your commercial every day, your mind will stay fresh and focused on your startup. When you take a day off, it's harder to get back to work the next day. Well, I do not promote that you never take your time off. Everyone needs a break.

On a vacation day or journey, pick a quick, small task where your brain thinks about the occupation. Then continue with your rest and reduction. Most people already work many hours, so I do not advise working more hours per week. Instead, work fewer hours, but feast them over seven instead of five days. As you complete a task every day, your brain stays absorbed and focused on your startup. At the same time, you will be burned out by dipping your daily hours less.

11. Focus on curating your relationships

Investigation has exposed that we act and think like the people we apply most of our time with. Choose your tutors wisely to use your associations. A mentor can greatly grow your efficiency and focus. 95% of mentees said they felt more inspired when reporting to a counsellor.

A counsellor can stimulate you to focus and realize your opening goals because you know someone is rereading your work. Your mentor is your duty companion. If you find yourself being abstracted, you can focus again by familiarizing yourself to telling your mentor that you were not positive.

LESS INVESTMENT

Business Invention

Early your own business can be risky. However, the risk decreases melodramatically if your business entails little economic venture from you. The beauty of having a low-investment is that you can test without the weight of having to be positive in the goods of your income (and not having to pay employees).

However, it is trying to say if a company will be successful, especially if your business has not been truly verified in your target market. That's why it's so important that you have the autonomy to take perils and make faults in a relatively low-input situation. If your corporate is steadily successful, you can think about the delay, make it a full-time job, and maybe even chartering people. Until then, focus on testing and correcting until you find a method that works. Here are some propositions for businesses that do not suffer high costs:

Business Ideas with Low Investment and High Returns

1. Wedding planner

Wedding is somewhat that is never off season. With only a few of your help and your mind, you can easily receive a lot. The best part of this commerce idea is that you have to mediate, give and make everything.

2. Technical Freelancer

If you have some of the qualities of geek in your blood and the knowledge in any software design language, you can easily be rented by position your CV and work experience (optional) on any website that hires freelancers. The funds will be nominal and occasionally nothing.

3. Gym or fitness center

We live in a world where we often overlook to take care of our bodies, which leads to a decline of physical disorder. To avoid this, we favor going to gyms or gyms. It's definitely a worthwhile business idea to start a gym with the compulsory minimum gear in a good place.

4. Yoga and meditation center

Nobody can lead a healthy life with this wearing timetable, exciting life and a lot of work stress. Your yoga and deliberation center will help people to scrap with all these unlimited problems. Separately from that, it's also a very money-spinning business idea. Funds will only be a good place and some workers (optional). You can also get another guide if you do not have yoga and meditation.

5. Mechanical / electrical work

The advance of today's cohort technologies needs many powered and electrical goods. Therefore, the edifice of a garage for the care of vehicles or the sale of electrical uses in the current time can be convenient. Though the business is allied with a certain sum of speculation, the returns are always higher.

6. E-commerce websites

Online shopping is the new age. It's the coolest way to buy the best invention from thousands of choices. All you need is a website, and the products you want to sell. It can be anything like jewelry, shoes or domestic items for everyday use.

7. Blogging

Happy writing is the term here. If you have gen of a specific area and a thirst for writing, start writing and appeal visitors with your script skills. There are many free blogging stands like Blogger, Word Press etc. and AdSense will help you.

8. Realtor / Broker

The cost of land-living increases daily and people do not find anyone to please their needs. Here, real land agents can help as an associate for judging the best deals. Being a dealer or broker is tremendously beneficial. You can set up a rate to find a possible buyer or search for the stuff you need. Only means of statement and language skills are compulsory to please customers and earn money.

9. Computer Trainer

In this world of computers, everybody needs to know at least the essentials of the computer. If you know something about it, you can teach the essentials to middle-aged and older people, or if you're a specialized expert, you can easily produce a lot from it.

10. YouTube channel

Everyone knows YouTube. There are many personalities who have become renowned because of YouTube. All you have to do is start a YouTube channel, create your own videos, and distribute. The videos can be from an amusement series or even lessons to anything. The more you upload, the more viewers you get and the more you earn with online promotion.

11. Cooking classes

Whether you are a housewife or a cooking fanatic, you can simply start it in your own kitchen with all your preferred recipes. It is not needed to participate a lot. Just start with your cooking class, buy groceries, do some marketing and start receiving.

12. Business Broker

This is the period for which there is no early speculation. Just like Quikr and eBay, get the persons who want to sell their used foodstuffs and attach them with those who want to buy those second-hand goods. Get the command if the deal is Exchanged.

13. Fast food restaurant

Grip a chair, get a chef (or cook yourself), develop a name, cook enchanting food and start grossing money. This is the lone business where you twitch grossing from day one and if clients like your food, you can effortlessly turn out to be an efficacious businessperson.

14. Driving school

The thoroughgoing aptitude compulsory for this business is the information of driving, and the concentrated outlay is an automobile. Demonstrate people to drive and twitch without making much.

15. Mobile Food Service

One or the other you advocate a restaurant or cook yourself. All you prerequisite is a delivery boy or more (contingent on the request) and automobiles. Give the facility on time and serve enjoyable food.

16. Recruitment services

You can start your private company, which deals with employment organizations for other businesses.

17. Organizer of the event

Opening a minor business establishing an occasion might be a decent idea, but this may necessitate unusual skills and individuals to do the same.

18. Social Media Services

Co-authoring for businesses, posting on blogs, Facebook, LinkedIn and Twitter accounts & Facebook pages.

19. Interior designer

The interior design business may be the finest pact, but this can necessitate unusual abilities.

20. Grocery

Food is the utmost desirable business for vending numerous goods that people want on a daily base. This is a lucrative business with no fatalities, as food is the rudimentary daily need of all individuals. You merely have to capitalize a few thousand to purchase a portfolio from a seller and sell it on the market. You can shop for each product traded. You can start after a mall in a mall and slowly increase as desirable.

21. Teaching / Coaching Course

Education will on no occasion sojourn. Today, owing to the strong competition, students preparing for competitive testing need prerequisite preparation guidelines to get tangled in coaching interiors. These coaching interiors are an ever minor outlay business with greater profits, which donates to the diffusion of information and trains students to clear competent exams. But, all you need to do is make certain that you have a painstaking acquaintance of the subject and explain the subject well to the students. Not solitary do you have to teach math or science, but if you are sports proficient, you can deed as a professional sports instructor.

22. Mobile Shop

Opening a trivial mobile store is a decent idea for small businesses with small investment.

23. Translation services

Specifying in one or two languages that you can declare confidently or employ other translators who speak more than a few languages.

24. Driving school

To start this business, you need a group of cars and a good squad of drivers who can explain driving.

25. Parking

A prodigious place for safe and protected parking is the finest deal.

26. Music / Dance lessons

If you can dance very well, you can jolt a dance academy that is a very decent business idea with a nominal budget. Many mothers are beholding for a good dance course for their children. In concurrence with the prior shop, music and dance classes are very prevalent. There is no category shortage from which to select. All you want is room for dance lessons and gadgets for music lessons. To decrease costs, teachers may request students to bring their personal musical instruments. Businesses of this kind gain adhesion over time. Resolution is of the greatest position.

27. Babysitter

If you flinch a baby business in the city, you will surely succeed.

28. Courier service

Numerous people today are observing for healthier delivery costs and more prompt delivery if you can accomplish it. This business is for you.

29. Packer and moving company

It's a business idea where furthermost of the customers come as of state-owned public service businesses.

30. Ice cream parlor

Beginning an ice cream shop is an alternative great business idea.

31. Freelancers

If you can program well, there are numerous websites accessible that will permit you to do freelance toil and get salaried for it.

32. Bookstore

The book devotee constantly buys numerous books and makes the idea of an original bookshop nice-looking.

33. Computer Trainer

Providing computer teaching can be a decent business idea to study about computer process, which is an obligation in today's world.

34. Yoga center

In today's traumatic life, many societies have a preference to opt for yoga.

35. Travel agency

Starting a travel agency is a good business prospect with little speculation.

36. Security or espionage agency

With snowballing security needs, you can twitch your own sanctuary agency.

An additional great method is to work as a detective.

37. Data Entry Services

Countless businesses today are making money on data entry so you might be capable to bid such facilities.

38. Resume Writer

If you can do a recommence well and have profound information about the subject, you can turn out to be a resume writer.

39. DJ Services

Business Invention

The disc jockey facility is the ground-breaking business notion of part-time. People are beholding for DJ numerous times. If you can grip music very well, you can astound this business

40. Music lessons

The music business may be a terribly profitable business. You'll create tons of cash in on this business. All you would like to capitalize is experience in music and a device like a piano or stringed instrument. If you do not have a building to open music categories, you'll open that category at your home. You'll use the empty garage to create a lesson; therefore, your students will learn well.

41. Web design

Web style services area unit currently needed. You merely have investments within the variety of a portable computer or a laptop and in web networks. Employment as an online steelier involves web design and content solely. You'll find this job a lot simple if you've got the information, experience, and knowledge during this field. You'll additionally work as a contract net designer reception. As individuals demand net style, such a large amount of individuals ask for and pay dearly for those that provide these services. However, this business doesn't need investment. Though your net development skills verify the amount of your salaries for your run.

42. Blogging

Blogging may be a business that may bring the North American nation a giant profit. Our investment is merely attainable within the type of writing a web log, an online association, and a portable computer or laptop. It's extremely easy; however, it will build a giant profit. If the web log you produce comes initially with Google, the blogger is often paid by Google. This can be extremely useful and simple to start out. Additionally, blogging is travel by many folks and that they build stolen property while not investment.

43. Affiliate Marketing

One company that's most popular nowadays is affiliate selling. No would like for prime investment, you'll be able to sell alternative people's merchandise and enough, then we have a tendency to get numerous commissions and profits. However, you'll be able to do that business and build a profit while not a headache.

44. Laundry

Laundry may be a business that's straightforward to handle and quickly reaches the general public market. Many folks square measure searching for these services for his or her everyday lives. The laundry business may be a business that suits you as a result of that you'll be able to use the washer and detergent alone. There square measure already several laundries that are flourishing. Does one wish to pursue your success? If thus, begin with this low investment business concept might bring you an enormous profit.

45. Online Shop

Many people favor to look within the on-line store. This can be as a result of they are doing not need to hassle to return to the shop to shop for one thing. You'll be able to simply get the merchandise you wish together with your phone and also the product can sink in at once. It's going to be a chance for you to try business within the space of the web store. You are doing not need to invest by shopping for merchandise, simply by marketing merchandise from others. Thus you'll be able to succeed in high profits.

46. Mobile / computer repair

Technology is essential nowadays. It is now a necessity and not a luxury. Repairing devices such as laptops and computers is a one-time investment. Take the necessary diploma/training and get your hands dirty. Every retailer selling cell phones and PCs has a small area for the repair work in the corner of his shop. No, you are not asked to sit there, but it is a plausible way to earn money.

47. Public Speaking Lessons

Stage fright may be a worry that strikes each individual. Some are born with the inherent ability to talk confidently; however, a number of North American nation lacks this ability in childhood. If you have got the flexibility to talk before an oversized audience, with clarity and magnificence that produces folks jealous, then this attribute will assist you to gain some Moolahs whereas up others' lives.

48. Writing content and copying content

Websites ought to have content to induce the much-needed traffic (yes, there square measure exceptions). Anyone UN agency feels that they're writing nice content will generate a secondary supply of financial gain by providing articles, columns, and different websites. The scale of the purchasers and therefore the quantity you receive per attribution is at first lower, however as presently because the flow sets in, the sky is the limit.

The basic demand is sound information of the language and its subtleties. And this should be supplemented with innovation and ingenuity.

49. Advice

The house includes agents that facilitate folks to get things done. A house reduces the employment of individuals and doesn't need investments with higher profits. The most effective example of a service is TATA in Bharat. The legal, monetary and technical diversity of the areas means it's best to generalize this broad class for this class. Expertise and success in your niche can confirm the profitableness you'll relish. A number of the popular rising consulting firms in Bharat are:

Consulting for digital marketing

With additional and additional folks logging on for the primary time and ranking the amount on Google, digital promoting consultation is usually high. With a decent data of computer program optimisation or social media, you'll be able to simply begin a DM firm and facilitate the corporate growth in no time.

Dietary counseling

With additional and further folks making an attempt to work and sensible than ever before, a dietary recommendation has become a crucial service. If you'll be able to learn nutrition diet and nutrition, you'll be able to keep cash with low investment. With additional and additional folks making an attempt to be work and sensible than ever before, dietary recommendation has become a crucial service. If you'll be able to learn nutrition diet and nutrition, you'll be able to keep cash with low investment.

BUSINESS ROADMAP

Business Invention

The business roadmap is comparable to a business arrangement. It offers you a protracted summary of wherever your organization is and the way to urge there. However, what's totally different from your typical business arrangement is that the visual image of your company at the next level.

This kind of roadmap exemplifies your organization's key goals and techniques for realizing development. Meant for corporations that accommodates manifold divisions, a corporate roadmap averts discrete clusters from becoming latched in via undoubtedly process longer term of the organization and also the role of every department for its future growth.

The growth of the corporate will currently be shown in several forms of roadmaps, eg; a tactical roadmap, a startup roadmap or perchance one thing sort of a selling or time unit roadmap. However, the foremost communal usage circumstance for charting corporate development might be a roadmap that envisages crucial enterprise development comes plus dates altogether departments of a business. Let's look into this instance for a business roadmap.

1. Create the Company Name

It's wonderful however necessary a reputation are often. It plays a monumental role within the growth and perception of a complete, which means that it will utterly produce or break a business. For any company whose name becomes an entrepreneurial milestone Apple, Uber, Google, etc. - there square measure uncounted names whose names don't properly mirror the complete, and also the company suffers. We all know the strength of a complete, and if a reputation is that the face of the complete, finding the proper name is crucial. Here is the reason.

    i.   It is the very first thing customers see.
    ii.   The entire relationships square measure determined by the primary impressions. Therefore, it's indispensable to induce a

robust impact like a shot. The primary factor a customer cooperates with might be present as a name; therefore, he has got to transfer the proper missive. It's en route to inspiring the spectators. Think about it as a primary handshaking. It says heaps regarding the person and makes a robust impression. "A likable, unique name will enable the customer to preserve in thoughts, and that we altogether try to be remarkable and maintain the customer - the tinier and calmer the sophisticated." Same Margot Bushnaq, founder and business executive of BrandBucket. A decent name has the facility to create an enduring relationship between a business and its customers, however on the opposite hand, it's the facility to ruin otherwise smart relationships.

iii. It sums up everything a corporation is regarding.
iv. Their square measure variety of things that compose the right name. It is not essentially the simplest strategy for a complete, if you investigate a corporation name from the pinnacle. It provides a spread of emotional incentives and establishes a corporation as an trade leader. "I keep in mind puzzling over it for weeks and hunting uncounted choices, and at last, my business partner Adam Topping, named CustomOnIt, place it during a shell that fantastically combines everything our company has to do." Co-owner Paul missionary explains, basically, it's AN unbelievably temporary outline of everything the business is regarding. Think about a number of the largest names within the world - let's visit Apple once more. The name has sure values and beliefs, and its complete is thereby consolidated. They have confidence quite simply their merchandise. They think about Steve Jobs, elegant style and also the like.
i. it's your distinctive approach to AN trade
ii. There square measure several firms in each trade. Even newer industries square measure quickly gaining in attractiveness and attract entrepreneurs, such a lot of firms provide similar

services to shoppers. Why do customers select one company over another? The character of a company; as Simon Sinek may say, her "why?" disapproval sells, and also the name sealed on a complete will most of the footwork.

iii. To place it merely, it's quite simply a reputation. It's the identity of an entire complete. It deserves time and a focus, and if done right, it'll amend a business forever.

2. Create a company logo

Your emblem is an important part of creating your whole a successful whole - with quality merchandise and positive referrals.

So, if you do not grasp why an emblem is therefore necessary, browse on to seek out out why.

"A strong logo is the beginning of your company's branding and communicates the vision of your company."

Grabs Attention

An emblem will quickly grab the eye of viewers and communicate the core values of a business in a stimulating method. This short span - you recognize, the one wherever customers decide your business by appearance - are often to your advantage if you've got a solid emblem that speaks to your business. It is the foundation of your brand identity

Successful stigmatization is regarding telling a story that influences the emotions of shoppers - plain and straightforward.

Even though the brand style is just a part of a company's whole, it is the muse for the whole narrative the whole builds upon. Colors, sounds, fonts - all of this is determined by the story you're trying to tell, and your logo is the stage for that story.

Business Invention

These elements will later be transferred from your logo to all of your branded materials - letterheads, business cards, landing pages, as you call them - creating a concrete, marketable brand identity

Promotes brand loyalty

As your whole grows, your emblem becomes higher known to a range of customers, and this familiarity creates the perception that your simple area unit sure and accessible.

Think about it: once you are out and close to obtain exercise article of clothing and suddenly discover track pants with the Greek deity swish, you'll look quickly. Why? As a result of which Greek deity article of clothing you recognize that your simple area unit in safe hands. Greek deity could be a whole you trust. Trust relies on a well-designed emblem, and whole loyalty follows quickly.

As before long as you wish them, your customers can keep coming to you - and your emblem is what they're trying to find 1st.

3. Select a product or service

To succeed as an associate businessperson, you need to develop the flexibility to pick and provide the correct product or services to your customers in a very competitive market. Over the other issue determines your ability to create that alternative, your success or failure.

Eighty p.c of the product and services consumed these days square measure totally different from those consumed 5 years past. And in 5 years, eighty p.c of the product used square measure new and totally different from those used these days.

Today, customers have access to thousands of product and services. And you've got unlimited opportunities to beat the market and effectively contend with a replacement product or service that's in some ways in which higher than what your competitors already provide. Bear in mind that your ability to decide on a product or service is crucial to your success.

The most vital issue you'll be able to do before deciding what you would like to sell is to assume. The lot of you think that a couple of product or service before you set it on the market, the higher your selections square measure.

4. Mission and vision

Whether you run a little one-woman business or an outsized business, a company mission and vision help to serve the workers. The mission And vision of a company are an integral part of company strategy as they serve to outline future goals and operational techniques. Though mission and vision are typically interchangeable terms, they really discuss with 2 totally different aspects of the business.

Understand mission statements

The mission statement of the organization describes the company's business, goals, and strategy for achieving those goals. It focuses a lot on wherever the corporate is presently situated and what military science steps it desires to require attaining its goals. The mission statement of an organization is often accustomed from the culture of the organization.

When you produce a mission statement for your business, describe what it will in your organization, World Health Organization you serve and the way you serve it. These are the 3 most significant components of a company mission statement. As an example, Amazon's mission statement is: "We need to supply our customers rock bottom doable costs, the simplest deals out there and also the highest level of comfort."

For example, if a little business sells camp-made baby garments, the mission statement can be, "We supply new oldster's lovely garments for his or her babies that are camp-made amorously." This conjointly includes what the corporate will, World Health Organization its audience is and the way it serves you. It provides staff a transparent goal.

Understand vision instructions

While the mission statement focuses on additional military science aspects of the corporate, the mission statement appearance in the long run of the corporate. The vision statement sets the direction within which the corporate needs to travel. In conjunction with the mission statement, it helps to form the structure strategy for the corporate.

Answer questions about your hopes and dreams once making a vision for your business. What future does one wish to ascertain and the way the corporate will play a task in achieving this? Square measure you trying to find an amendment, and the way one does it? Amazon's vision is, "To be the foremost customer-focused company within the world wherever customers will realize and see everything they require to shop for on-line." It offers workers a transparent direction.

For the tiny company manufacturing hand-made baby garments, a vision would possibly be: "To be the primary selection for brand spanking new oldsters WHO wish to equip their babies with hand-made, overseen vesture that has been designed and made with nice attention to detail." The corporate needs to travel into the long run and the way it needs to attain this standing. It conjointly contains its main point.

5. Investment size and why you need this money, where you want to invest

Many people prorogue the investment as a result of the suppose they have heaps of cash - thousands of bucks to speculate. That is simply not true. You'll begin finance as very little as $ fifty a month.

The key to putting together prosperity is to develop smart habits - like hard cash often on a monthly basis. If you create a habit currently, you're in a very a lot of stronger money scenario on the road.

Here are 5 ways in which you'll invest with slight cash:

Go for the cookie jar

Saving cash and investment is closely amalgamated. To speculate cash, you need to 1st save one thing. It takes a lot of but you're thinking that, and you'll get it on in terribly petite paces.

If you've never been a saver, you'll begin storing simply $ ten every week. That doesn't seem to be a lot of, however over a year, it's over $ five hundred. Marcus Bank presently offers a powerful APY of 2.25% for its on-line bank account. There's no minimum deposit or monthly maintenance fee related to a Marcus bank account, that the come back on all credits is earned.

The complete conjointly offers high-yield CDs and a spread of loans if you're within the marketplace for an area wherever you'll park your cash or if you wish some capital.

Try to place $10 in a sachet, shoebox, minor safe, or feasibly the mythological seat of the principal alternative, the container. While this can sound senseless, it's characteristically a compulsory inaugural change. Get familiarized living a trace, but you be and retain the investments in a very nonviolent place. The electronic corresponding of the biscuit cans is the online investments account; it is distinct from your testing account. The money can be introverted inside two business days if you prerequisite it, but it is not knotted to your debit card. If the standard is then an adequate amount, you can yield it out and transfer it into some real speculation apparatuses.

Flinch with slight sums of money and then upsurge as you turn out to be more gratified with the progression. It might be a matter of determining not to go to McDonald's or pass the movies on and in its place put that money in the cookie jar.

Would you like the money to be capitalized instantly? Acorns is an app that abridges your credit and debit card acquisitions and capitalizes the alteration. It's not decorative, but it's a twitch. And for persons who have never been investors, the twitch is even more significant.

2. Let a Robo Advisor invest your money for you

Robo consultants are produced to create investment as straightforward and reachable as attainable. No preceding speculation proficiency is needed, and therefore the setup is straightforward. Allow your machine-driven info track your investments whereas paying lowerfees.

Wealth before

An unlimited robo mentor I like to endorse for depositors for the main time is Prosperity Front.

Your fees are reasonable at zero.25%, however the football player is that you just will achieve your initial $ five,000 without charge (specific to MU30 readers).

So if you would like to venture with very little cash, Prosperity Front may be the cheers to go. However, you may like $ five hundred to start out the prosperity front. Remember.

M1 finances

If you are not having an opening stability of $ five hundred, there are still nice selections within the Robo informatory space.

There are not any instructions or management fees for money source Economics, and therefore the least balance is purely $ a hundred.

You can select among one in every of their pre-built extensive collections or modify your own by shopping for frameworks and ETFs finished their stand. The border is tremendously forthright to use.

Improvement

If you initiate at but $ a hundred, think about retaining Improvement, as there's no least beginning balance.

Like M1, it's conjointly dreadfully suitable for trainees because it offers a really easy stage and a hassle-free speculation method.

Swelling

If it is vigorous for you to venture during an informally responsible way, effort Swell venture.

They even have an infrequent least (only $ 50) and ne'er capitalize in trades like oil, tobacco, weapons or non-public prisons.

Instead, they need modified renewable energy selections, inexpert technologies, sickness destruction, clean water, and more.

3. Log in to your employer's retirement plan

If you've got a skillful budget, even the forthright step of registration in your 401 (k) or another leader departure plan could seem unbearable. However, there's some way throughout which you'll be able to capitalize in subordinate employer-sponsored departure version that's thus little that you just don't even announce it.

For example, agree to capitalize just one choice of your pay within the leader position.

You probably won't even miss such a little influence, though what's even easier is that the inference you obtain for it'll generate the influence even lower.

Once you plan to a one pick influence, you'll be able to increase it incrementally annually. For example, within the second year, you'll be able to increase your influence to a duo of choice of your pay. Inside the third year, you'll be competent to upsurge your influence to pick of your pay so on.

If you schedule the rise with the yearly wage increase, you'll mark the overstated contribution even less. So, if you receive and a pair of the wage increase, the rise can effectively be divided between your departure version and your bank account. And if your leader makes associate acceptable contribution, the arrangement is even higher.

Tint could be a great instrument for the utilitarian speculation organization of your 401 (k) . You'll collect a free 401 (k) study, wherever you identify wherever and the way to enhance your venture. If you choose to use your facilities, you'll be emotional a reasonable quantity of $ ten per month.

4. Put your money in investment funds with low initial investment

Mutual assets are venture refuges that allow you to capitalize on a range of stocks and links in a solitary contract, making them perfect for new investors.

The unruly is that many mutual fund corporations need a least early venture of between $ 500 and $ 5,000. If you are a depositor for the first time and need to capitalize little money, these modicum may be unachievable. However, some mutual fund companies will relinquish the least quantities if you decide between $ 50 and $ 100 impulsive monthly savings.

Involuntary formation is common for mutual funds and ETF IRA accounts. For assessable accounts, this is less common, but it's always value asking if it's obtainable. Among the well-known fund businesses contain Dreyfus, Transamerica, and T. Rowe Price.

A mechanical investment contract is particularly beneficial if you can do it through investments in the workforce. Classically, you can set up an involuntary pay-in condition through your payroll, like to an employer-sponsored pension plan. Just ask your HR division about the setup.

Play it safe with Treasury Securities

Not many minor depositors start their venture voyage with US Treasury securities, but you can. You will never get ironic with these safeties, but it's a brilliant residence to park your money - and earn attention - until you're ready to invest in higher-risk, higher-yielding savings.

Treasury securities, also known as savings promises, can be easily acquired through the US Treasury Treasury Direct pledge gateway. There you can buy safe revenue US government safeties with adulthoods of 30 days to 30 years and a look value of $100.

You can also use Treasury Direct to buy inflation-protected refuges or TIPS. These not only wage attention but also occasionally regulate wealth to imitate surge due to variations in the shopper price index.

As with mutual funds, you can also place for your Treasury Direct version to be subsidized by pay reserves.

6. Study on competitors

One of the main influences in the permanency of a startup is the unceasing study and assessment of the struggle. Gaining the smallest edge on your competitors can make the difference between failure and success.

An astute entrepreneur knows that it's more than just a good business idea and funding to start a commercial. All rudiments contain the search of the market. This includes appraising the assets and faintness of the struggle. Research is a vital part of every new occupational. To make sure that there is a real market for your future occupation, you must also appreciate the market portion of your entrants.

There are some best practices to get the information you need to know if your commissioning is a viable option.

Judgment of your competitors

If you want to find material about your participants, start with an operational check-in at Corporations House. All partial obligation corporations in the United Kingdom must catalogue with Companies House. Material about more than three million British corporations is reserved. Many of the corporation particulars are easily obtainable, but for the least charge of £ 1.00, you can gather supplementary substantial. Available participant facts may contain the countryside of the commercial, insolvency particulars, business accounts, annual returns, and existing agendas.

Online sources of information for companies

The Internet is one of the premium tools to fold struggle information about the competition. When you know where to look, you can easily admit key commercial material to improve vision into how your contestants contest in the marketplace. You can find material about contestants on websites such as Linkedin, Pipl, Tour Mentor and ZoomInfo. Do not overlook to exploration for material on your participant's existing website, as well as communal interacting sites such as Facebook and Twitter to instrument their status and purchaser response.

7. Plan marketing strategy:

Business Invention

Startups presence many tasks, but not as unwarranted or severe as trying to stay confident. The Marginal Business Development Agency (MBDA) approximations the normal charge of initial an occupation at about $ 30,000. There are notable differences in this numeral, with selected businesses initial for a few hundred dollars and others requesting more than millions.

But reminisce: these statistics are just startup prices. In total, new companies have to pay thousands of lineup incomes, agency rental dues, raw supplies, and other constant effective outlay each month, while stressed to make enough to stay awash.

Most tycoons who are in this bad monetary opposite act finish up with reserves that are deliberate pointless, such as promotion and upgrading. The punishing irony, however, is that deserting advertising as a whole deters a corporation's progress, consequential in less income and the need to chance the money into an even more obstructive cheap.

About 80 percent of businesspersons do not know how to amount the efficiency of promotion policy. No wonder advertising becomes into the ax so fast.

Here's the point: Active promotion does not have to price a lot of money. Sure, higher-budget promotion policies can bring more discernibility and steadiness to probable returns, but there are many very actual and cost-effective advertising tactics to help you get started. Here are nine of them:

References

One of the finest ways to market is to totally evade advertising. In its place, make a scheme that lets your clienteles do the advertising for you. Deliberate the fact that people purchase produce four times more frequently when advanced by a colleague.

Notwithstanding the newspaper of practical magazines, we still trust overhead all on individual references. In adding, scenery up a transfer package does not charge much, and contingent on the construction, the database is wholly free. You could give your present patrons a concession on their donations if you denote a new purchaser or proposition a cash bonus if you really capitalize on that policy. Just make sure you inform your patrons (possibly using one of the other approaches listed below).

Press releases and news features

People read the newscast frequently, and if you have somewhat new to report, most news activities will be happy to report it to you. Press releases are a lucrative way to indicate your produce in vital magazines and perhaps find some inward relatives along the way. If you do all the work yourself and quest down Medias and direct e-mails, press statements can actually be a free promotion policy.

Otherwise, you might wage a few hundred dollars to get an announcement syndication through an ability like PR Newswire. If you are only attentive in being referenced, visit Assistance a Writer Out (HARO) and stretch the medias tips that are just to come for them.

Content Marketing

Content promotion has many procedures, but none necessitate important speculation. The calmest way to accomplish a blog on the crushed is to add new satisfied certain eras a week to update and amuse your readers in an exclusive and expedient way.

Info graphics, videos, and podcasts are also in the satisfied advertising grouping. Aim? All of these satisfied broadcasting can augment your variety standing, surge incoming circulation, and accompaniment the many other policies you pull out of this list (as you'll see).

SEO

If you devote time script traineeships for your satisfied promotion movement, you can also capitalize on improving your hunt train optimization (SEO).

New to SEO? It may appear theoretically compound, but the realism is, with some understanding and devotion, you can easily comprehend the fundamentals. You use online tools, such as Moz's Keyword Traveler, to classify applicable keywords that could lead to weighty circulation to your place if your brawl is low. You then adapt your website to contain those keywords.

You also necessity to make physical vicissitudes, reliably write superiority gratified and backlinks to your field. It's a lot of work, but if you do it yourself, it only takes time - which is price it, because the long-term welfares are massive.

Social Media Marketing

Social media selling is not approximately; you cannot do nonchalantly, but it's spontaneously existing. It's rather you can master when you participate time. Start producing outlines for your corporate on key podia like Facebook, Twitter, and Instagram. Work out your shapes; and start syndicating your satisfied target marketplace wants.

Contact persons and stay related. Over time, you could entice thousands of viewers on behalf of a commentator brook to your website.

E-mail marketing

Email advertising remains one of the most lucrative advertising policies, with some foundations demanding reappearance on speculation (ROI) of 400 percent or more. As long as you have a decent list (curated gradually slightly than believed) and a steady but non-invasive brook of outbound email blasts, you should be able to make a generous reoccurrence at any time and at any time you capitalize to attain a return.

PPC ads

Pay-per-click ads can be luxurious when directing complex keyword keywords. However, there are places and stages that are appropriate even for the most budget-conscious startup businessperson. For example, on Facebook, you can only salary $ 1 per day for positive ads (though you'll perhaps want to participate a little more if you want important consequences).

Personal branding

Personal marking works much like company marking, excluding that it smears to you as a separate. They promote themselves and their knowledge in social media and perhaps in an unusual blog to advance new factions and a diverse source of traffic and notice.

The price here is that persons are more likely to faith people than businesses, so in conclusion, you have a discrete, commanding way to association your satisfied or gain new leads - all without reimbursing a penny.

Forums and Groups

Do not undervalue the influence of prowling in community media and community media groups. You may see somebody asking a query that you can respond (with your knowledge), or you can acquire about the influence of an on-site occasion that you can use to endorse your business. The more you are linked to your particular civilizations, counting your district and wider manufacturing, the more you can win.

Best of all, it typically prices nobody to develop an associate of these societies so you can take benefit of them in just a few hours of your time.

The snack here? If you are harassed with your business's cheap, you should not unhinge promotion. In its place, find imaginative ways to realize gratitude of your variety and crops that do not necessitate important speculation.

8. Business Projection:

Generating monetary forecasts for your startup is both an art and knowledge. While savers want to see cold, firm numbers, it can be problematic to forecast your monetary presentation three years later, particularly if you still have seed wealth existing. Notwithstanding, short and average term monetary plans are a necessary part of your business plan if you want serious depositor courtesy.

The economic part of your occupational plan should hold a sales prediction, an expenditure economical, a cash flow statement, a balance sheet, and a revenue and loss version. It is imperative to fulfil with commonly recognized secretarial principles (GAAP) of the Monetary Office Morals Boarding, a private- law body accountable for situation secretarial and reportage ethics in the United States. If economic commentary is new land for you, have a book audit run your plans.

Sales forecast

As a startup corporation, you do not have to appraisal old results, which can make it hard to estimate income. However, it is likely to comprehend well the market you are incoming and the industrial drifts as a whole. In fact, income estimates based on a solid sympathetic of manufacturing and market leanings show possible depositors that they have done their homework and your prediction is more than just conjecture.

In practice, your prediction should be broken down into once-a-month sales, with admissions presentation which components are being vended, which price points and how many auctions you imagine. From

Business Invention

the second year of your business plan and outside, it is satisfactory to lessen the estimate to trimestral auctions. In fact, this is the circumstance for most rudiments of your business plan.

Expense budget

What you sell has to custody approximately, and in that inexpensive, you have to show your expenditures. In totaling to outlays, this encompasses the charge of units vended to your commercial. It's a decent impression to disruption depressed your incidentals into immovable costs and mutable costs. For example, influenced expenditures are the same or almost the same every month, counting rent, assurance, and others. Some values are likely to vary from month to month, e.g., B. by publicity or cyclical sales aids.

Cash Flow Statement

As with your income estimate, you need to do homework for the money current reports for a startup because you cannot use ancient statistics as an orientation. In small, this declaration cracks how much money activities into your occupational scheduled, or how much it undertakes. By using your income predictions and employ reasonable, you can shrewdly guess your cash flow.

Keep in mind that auctions often leave sales, contingent on the kind of occupation you're employed in. For example, if you have agreements with clienteles, they may not wage for the matters they buy pending the month after distribution. Some patrons may motionless have recognition poises 60 or 90 days after transport. You need to take this suspension into explanation when you calculate exactly when you expect your sales.

Income statement

Your P & L declaration should use the material from your income forecasts, expenditure cheap, and cash flow declaration to compute

Business Invention

how much you imagine to earn or lose in the three years comprised in your commercial plan. You should deliver a numeral for each discrete year and the complete three-year retro.

Balance Sheet

You deliver a citation of all your possessions and obligations in the equilibrium sheet. Many of these properties and accountabilities go yonder once-a-month incomes and incidentals. For example, any stuff, gear or unsold routine you own is a benefit with a cost that can be given to it. The same smears to unpaid invoices not billed to you. Even if you have no cash in hand, you can count these bills as properties. The quantity you owe from a business advance or the quantity you owe to others from voluntary bills would be careful obligations.

Balance is the alteration between the worth of all you own and the value of all you owe.

Break-even projection

If you have well predictable auctions and expenditures and arrived the numbers into a worksheet, you should be able to regulate a date on which your commercial disruptions, in other arguments, the day on which you develop lucrative and more cash Making It Out As a startup business, this is improbable to occur instant, but probable depositors want you to have a year in mind and that you can sustain that prediction with the statistics you've stated in the fiscal piece of your occupational plan.

Additional tips

When amassing your fiscal predictions, keep in attention some general tips:

- Acquaint yourself with the worksheet software if you are not already doing so. It is the starting point for all financial forecasts and provides flexibility so you can speedily change

Business Invention

expectations and evaluate alternate set-ups. Microsoft Excel is the most shared, and you possibly previously have it on your computer. You can also buy singular software posts to help with monetary growth.

- Prepare a five-year forecast. Do not comprise them in the profitable plan, because they added your system into the imminent, the steadier it is to estimate them. However, keep the prognosis complete in case a stockholder asks for it.
- Offer only two states. Depositors want a best-case state and a worst-case state, but should not deluge your commercial plan with innumerable mid-range states. They may only cause misperception.
- Be serviceable and sturdy. As already stated, fiscal estimating is as much art as knowledge. You have to receive convinced gears, such as your sales growth, how your rare substantial and organizational budgets will growth, and how successfully you gather your entitlements. It is best to be representative in your prognoses when irritating to beginner stockholders. If your commerce is moneymaking through a narrowing chapter and you suppose income development of 20 out of a hundred per month, you expect savers to see red flags.

9. SWOT analysis

The SWOT study is a planned preparation technique that events the possessions, weakness, probabilities, and jeopardizes a business or occupational start-up. This embraces scenery the corporation's goal or amalgamation and classifying the inner and outside factors that are promising and negative to completing that goal.

A SWOT examination initiates with the description of an anticipated closing state or goal. In an original promotion plan for opening an occupation, the anticipated final status or goal is likely to consequence in promotion goals being met after one year.

The documentation of SWOTs is significant because the ladders in the arrangement procedure to influence the nominated mark can be derivative from the SWOT investigation.

The four dissimilar issues in the SWOT examination are defined as:

- Strengths: Qualities of the society that are obliging in realizing the goal
- Weaknesses: Qualities of the society that harm the attainment of the goal
- Opportunities: Outside circumstances that are obliging in realizing the goal
- Threats: Outside circumstances that may affect the presentation of the business

Examples of assets physiognomies that can be used to give the business a modest benefit may include:

- Copyrights
- Robust trademark names
- Decent status between clients
- Price recompenses done own know-how
- Beneficial manufacturing opportunities
- Larger supervise
- Inexpensive contact to dispensing systems
- Larger merchandise
- A larger place where the merchandise can be obtained
- Marketing profits such as marketing, community affairs, word of mouth and point of sale

Your company benefits from its strengths

A faintness can be distinct as the absenteeism of inexpensive asset such as:

- Absence of obvious defense
- A feeble product name
- Immoral status between patrons
- High price construction
- Absence of admittance to decent incomes or normal possessions
- Absence of admittance to main circulation networks

Your company will support its weaknesses

The examination of the outside situation can expose income and evolution chances for the startup occupational. Some of them are:

- A displeased purchaser prerequisite
- Reduction of guidelines
- A mounting market section
- Technical variation
- Socio-cultural variations

Your company will use its strengths to invest in its opportunities

Outside conservational intimidations can be the supplementary side of opportunities. These can include:

- Undesirable socio-cultural variations
- Technical variations that is kinda merchandise outdated
- Dangers from variations in rules and instructions
- shifting the tastes of consumers from the company's products
- Improved barricades to the profession

10. Franchise model

Permitting your profitmaking is an established way to cultivate fast. However, becoming a franchisor is not an involuntary voucher to victory, particularly in this stimulating frugality. Three reputable franchisors trailed for insolvency in January: Taco Del Mar Permitting Corp., Uno Restaurant Possessions Corp. and Daphne's Greek Café.

Nonetheless, countless businesspersons vision of making their brand a domestic name, with a linkage of authorizations from coastline to coastline or round the biosphere. If the correct idea is applied efficiently, it can be a countless growth approach that does not require an abundant blunt principal as company-owned entities do.

If you are in view of franchising, you must know that the franchisor procedure is typically extensive and experiences noteworthy prices. Just since you succeed for permit auctions does not mean that you will discover purchasers. Statistics from the Intercontinental Franchise Suggestion display that out of the 105 businesses that started vending franchises in 2008, further than 40 did not shoot the sale of their first element by the conclusion of 2009.

To turn into an effective new franchisor, you prerequisite to make several considerate verdicts timely that will have an emotional impact on your corporate. At hand are also a lot of authorized leaflets that you want to form to make certain your company obeys with national and state commandments leading the franchise trade.

At this juncture is our escort to the significant ladders you prerequisite to take to grow into an innovative franchisor.

Know your business inside and out.

The directives providing to every franchisee necessity maybe precise. Nevertheless, businesspersons are frequently familiarized to intuitional dynamism of their businesses, and it can be problematic for them to express all the insignificant but vital promises they achieve each day. Franchisees will not have the liberty to make up, and their necessity be expressed on how to do the whole thing from book-keeping to assembling goods. Each stage of the procedure requisite to be prudently drawn. The businessperson might prerequisite to revive what it's like to track business for the major time.

Tariq Farid had four flower sprees till he was nineteen. He reminisces meeting with his mother who facilitated him in the store once he ended sixty dollars a day, and he would articulate her about his fantasy of producing seventy-one day. When he grasped his journey's end, he arrived one more fantasy. Soon he stated his mother that he sought to make eight or nine thousand dollars a day. "It not once finishes," he utters.

For Farid, CEO and originator of Comestible Preparations This early knowledge was healthier for Farid than any corporate school, but it ensured not to make him ready for the defies, the subsequent impression, a business that vended garlands of imprinted garden-fresh fruit, into an intercontinental franchise take along. When he underway, franchising was not fragment of his business idea. "We fixated largely on constructing the trade," speaks Farid. Which means that no occupation was as well small for Farid to receive himself. Once the company's website wanted photographs of the manufactured goods, Farid turn into an unprofessional snapper. When his trade needed a more vigorous backend to handgrip extra briefings online, Farid made it.

Farid articulates he did not reason much around franchising once he originated into his workshop one day and thought he sought to build-up an appetizing preparation in Boston. To understand what might have tangled opening a franchise, Farid decided to organize a trial course himself in the practice of a subsequent store. He brings into being a edifice, marched the documents, and went over all the minutia himself, from embellishing the inside to teaching the team. He enforced himself to go over and done with every stage of the procedure precisely as an innovative franchisee would.

Notify yourself about the legal questions.

Mulgannon counsels all business proprietors wanting to cross the threshold to the franchise industry to fulfil with argument 19 of their FDD submission. At this juncture, a franchisor delivers monetary evidence. Mulgannon utters that if somewhat is erroneous with Article 19 of a business, he will reject to toil with them. These lawful difficulties are one zone in which the expectant franchisor pursues specialized assistance.

Farid would not counsel anybody to franchise deprived of proficient guidance. "I ensured it frequently for myself," Farid articulates of his initial labors to nurture money, halt the lawful jungle, and agreed up his grievance. "We partook no money, and it remained problematic to verve to a bank with a fruit carrier."The one advisor Farid has inadvertently placed the determined businessperson on the accurate passage." I went to this mentor and offered me a mandible, he said it would charge $ 100,000, "says Farid Farid stated the counsellor he cannot." I cannot manage to pay for that. "I ponder he alleged flippantly," Why do not you attempt it by hand? "I appropriated him earnestly, I did not ponder he'd kidded." Farid speaks he prepared a lot of errors, and in conclusion he employed franchising advisors, but by that period he had erudite a lot himself.

The Intercontinental Franchise Connotation is also an outstanding reserve when it approaches lawful franchising subjects. The IFA accumulates statistics on franchise businesses, indorses rules that are promising to franchises, and delivers capitals and support to businesses that want to develop franchisees. The association also issues gossips on the franchising laws, counting an overview of the franchising commandment. Whether a fascinated small commercial man thrives in cultivating over the reread second version of 450 sheets can in himself be an inspection of the principle of a businessperson.

Know how you want to grow.

Business Invention

The clue of development is tempting, but a minor occupational wants their business to gauge at a rational price. For some businesses that need to develop franchises, the new occupational may mean growing coast-to-coast growth worldwide. For others, it may mean adding a minority of new openings. The specialists endorse rising at the usual development rate for your business.

When a business derives to Mulgannon to discover the latent of permitting, they first sit down with them and sensibly inspect their resistant of the idea. "Before I can start with somebody or rent him as a client, I have to take my own care to make sure my eyes are wide open."

If an authorization is to cultivate, Mulgannon said, they would have to deliberate where their commercial perfect will work and how far they can swell their product into unacquainted land. He operated with a business called Erik's DeliCafe, a popular sandwich shop and caterer in Northern California. The company has a firm product consciousness in California and numerous adjacent states, and with Mulgannon's help, they obvious to swell in California and northern Nevada. They have mature, but within their product consciousness.

The other danger is global licensing, something that Mulgannon has discovered with Junk King. "I've contracted a contract with a Panamanian speculation collection to progress Junk King across Central America," says Mulgannon. "They arose to see us, and I paid twelve days there transferring a worldwide principal license." Mulgannon is self-assured that this deal will allow Junk King to extend its product outside the US with negligible risk.

Check your franchisee.

That somebody needs to open a permit with the designation of your business does not mean that you must let him. They will characterize your product, so make sure you have an organization that will guarantee that you are pouring your business in the right course in a new market.

Farid says he has a way of significant if somebody is manufacturing a good franchisee. "I used to appeal it the Googledy Eye Test, if somebody came up to me and said," I want to construct a franchise, I think it will be great! "And they did not recognize the hard effort," Farid says he would occur.

Eagerness is as mutual in permitting as it is in any occupational. In accumulation to the documents and commercial material of possible franchisees, so Mulgannon, he takes into explanation the characters of businesspersons. Like Farid, he does not want somebody who has all desire, but no matter. Better that they are considerate, diffident and excited about their commercial. "Most permit businesses are being propelled with a shotgun methodology," Mulgannon says of his methodology to client collection. "Often they are sold to everyone, that's a big mistake."

"We get about 20 requirements a day and we eradicate about 75 percent of them," says Mulgannon. "Most people are observing for a work where they can work on the truck." Mulgannon labelled junk kings more as a worker franchise. Contrary to what you might imagine, Junk King is not absorbed in franchisees who are mainly fascinated in setting on labor gloves and receiving into the truck. Mulgannon says he and his worker are looking for data delivered by candidates in the search for precise potentials. "One of the big displays for us is the earlier pay prospects," says Mulgannon. "If you want to swap six digits, that's good for us."

Determine the correct restrictions.

Even if franchisees are assumed very exact commands on insolences, exercise and other performs, there will be, and should be, convinced independence they should have. They are also small occupational landlords, and if the franchisor starts receiving out of the day-to-day commercial, he or she will have to trust on the ruling of the franchisees as they discover new occupational occasions. Give them freedoms, but keep these liberties restricted.

Diverse permissions have changed thoughts about the limitations they want to execute on their franchisees. They are stressed to reunite upholding product character with the traces and sentiments of each contract landlord. Mulgannon says he declined a contract that required help to develop a permit because they would usual very close-fitting restrictions on who might become a franchisee. "The supplies for the franchisee would have been far too firm," Mulgannon said. "The pool of franchisees would have been far too small."

Brand development is always the final goal, says Mulgannon. One obligation that Junk King makes to all franchisees is that they spend the least quantity on marketing, whether it be TV, radio, print or any other average. "They have to capitalize ten percent of their uncultured income back into their marketplace," says Mulgannon. Junk King offers about 90 percent of the obligatory promotion physical, and corporations can have other ideas accepted by the company office.

Support your franchisees.

Even if the franchisor twitches to move away from license commercial, he or she should apply additional time receiving to know the franchisee.

A franchisee is dissimilar from other types of small commercial proprietors. He has opened a new occupational or a new facility breadwinner and is accountable for presentation in a precise area. He or she lives off the commercial and supervises all day-to-day processes. However, there is continuously a larger occupational construction, and the franchisee works within that construction from license to franchise.

A license model grants some precise tasks because when the occupational is good and new industries are unbolted, the business is always employed with new people. Farid says Edible Provisions has a subdivision that works with permissions to get their supplies. Another is exercise and other worries about conceivable difficulties, unpredicted variables of any caring. To guarantee that all mechanisms replace calm, constant communication is required. "We will spend a lot of time communicating connected with them [franchisees] about what's going on this week, what the tests are and where to look for them," says Farid.

Farid says his personnel occasionally say he's too suspicious, too floppy. The boy, who required finding a way to sell more long-stemmed roses, still finds it problematic to crinkle his smock at the finish of the day. It was not pending Essible Preparations reached 500 or 600 supplies that he acquired a step back, says Farid. "I still visit the stores because I value that the most," he says. "In addition, when you become to the size we have now, the franchisees have selected you to start the next big thing." Farid would not divulge what the next prospect could be for edible provisions. But he would say the quest never ends.

COLLECT DATA

Business Invention

It is a mutual delusion among small commercial proprietors that they do not essentially need to assign a position to figures assortment and construction of a workflow for selling with facts that goes to and from their commercial. Most of them have quickly disregarded the need for a prepared and effectual data-processing and gathering course due to the extent of their occupational. This is frequently due to the misunderstanding that statistics narrates only to the "big data" debated so often, which are fast in standing for huge manufacturing or companies.

The circumstance is, every business assembles data irrespective of its size. If you cooperate with patrons, accept outgoings from them, and keep a list of signal about them, you already have data.

Statistics is material - in simple and simple words.

And how you gather material - data - and use it for your occupational can validate the accomplishment or letdown of your occupational. Black Inventiveness came up with a list of motives why small productions would amass data for two reasons:

1) better know customers to meet their desires, 2) drive growth for the occupational, and be able to make conversant business choices and to type approaches.

For small industries, however, data collection can be crushing. Most only, they do not know how or where to jump, especially how they use the composed data for analysis.

We have industrialized five best performs for management data collection competently for your small business:

1. Specify a procedure or workflow.

First of all, you need to generate a process that permits data gathering to be achieved faultlessly, frequently, and proficiently by somebody who is tasked with it. Keep it simple. It does not have to be seriously planned. A file can be as simple as an Excel database covering the main list of purchaser material. Make it work that it's easy to inform, reread, and orient at any time. Your course should also grow with your occupational, so you do not have to acquiesce a new one each month.

2. Master the procedure.

After you have set up the workflow, you must master it. Keep doing. Be dependable with it. You need to master the course so that you can examine its efficiency and make variations from there. Appraise and advance the procedure unceasingly until you make it perfect for your commercial. Data assortment depends more on developments and administration - it is not a short-term development. You partake to work continuously to be able to work proficiently.

3. Only collect what is important for your business.

Keep it humble again. It's so easy to collect evidence these days - with the Internet and how we can hoax clienteles into if more material than essential, which is the circumstance with giant suggestions and capacities of an auction, concession or handout. But think about it - will it help your salable now or in the upcoming?

A typical example: Most small industries twig to the greatest repetition of amassing facts from patrons - pen and paper; Fill out methods. And that's okay. But what would you do with these identifications after you have scrambled the figures material? Do not strain too much about the requirement to maintain it. Except it is a legal document, it is improved to stay away from the mess. You now have the electric files. All you have to do is make sure your electric files stay safe and secure.

4. Store the collected data in a safe place.

Business Invention

Electronic archives have extremely condensed book-keeping and litter in offices. It has even enhanced corporate acts, given how speedily desired evidence can be edited by everybody who needs it.

These welfares include dangers. Data obstacles advanced more joint even in small trades. In fact, small trades are a target for hackers who can pierce larger businesses.

Small commercial possessors need to have safety payments on their system (or on a solitary mechanism if they have one). Not only do you have to often check your IT network, but also who is retrieving your documentation. Personnel can also be a susceptible place for data openings. You can even be the one who bargains your evidence if you are not careful.

In cunning to safety, settling the uprightness of your computer hardware is also mandatory. The loss of files may occur due to a failure of the device. Make sure your hard drives and files are not hurt.

5. Rent outside the company.

You tried to create a sequence, and someway it motionless does not work for you. Relax. There is one more solution: subcontracting. Small industries can save a lot of money by subcontracting part of their corporate - and data assortment is one of them.

When you subcontract, you will assign your data gathering to a club of experts who knows how to create a workflow and mature a folder for your commercial. They will detain the data you receive - from patrons, contractors, buyers, etc. and establish them in habits that will be accommodating to your commercial. They can also communicate you how to preserve then study it.

When you think about it, you can suggestively progress your occupational by reorganization the assemblage of your numbers. You can use it to produce more income for your corporate. It all starts with receipt to know your clients healthier, what they want and essential, if replies for what they necessity, and thus if a better connection that tips to devotion.

Keep in mind that statistics cluster can only be valuable if you can treasure a way to make it exertion for your commercial. By subcontracting or subsequent the best performs drew above, you've originated one step earlier to calculating for your business.

Careful investigation is serious to the enterprise of many advertising and publicity resources for your objective market, taking into description their needs and the benefit of their contestants. We can help you grow inclusive approaches through in-depth study services that are sensibly made-to-order to your direct occupational needs.

Market research:

Ads and publicity solid flow online and offline to your patrons each day. This services dealers appreciate their regulars, their bazaar, and their contestants. Market study is not just a way to attain this, but above all, to make well-versed promotion results. Market study also gives advertising specialists a well-thought-of intellect of what's going on or what's likely to occur, liable on how patrons perform in their current promotion labors.

With an infinite sum of figures always being existing in a world where evidence can become archaic in a single day, finding a regular way to appreciate everything becomes a prime and crucial tricky for a vendor. After all, this evidence has a huge effect on purchaser performance and your corporation's skill to realize it. This is where subcontracting twitches.

Infinit Datum's subcontracted investigation facilities offer a cost-effective answer to the boring job of probing from deposit to coating of raw evidence. Our subcontracted study services will help you complete all of your market research capabilities by adding progressive standpoint and classifying sightless spots or likely prejudices in your advertising doings from a third-party viewpoint.

Our subcontracted investigation amenities offer a varied choice of measurable and qualitative bazaar investigation examination devices tailor-made to your corporate needs. Over the years, we have acknowledged uncountable marketplace study tasks for clients in a variety of industries, including technology, healthcare, social media, and even the motorized business, to term but a few. Our accrued first-hand knowledge in these varied trades gave us admission to the essential marketplace evidence and the skill to repeatedly familiarize to the requirements of our patrons.

Our team is made up of conversant, dependable and practical specialists with years of involvement and expert gen of the up-to-date business trends.

Difficulties with concealment and material sanctuary ought not to be a delinquent at Infinit Datum because we feel stanch to defending you and your patron gen. This is extremely entrenched in our strategies and actions, as deep-rooted by the ISO 27001: 2005 Info Security Management System certification, which goals to guarantee Infinit Datum's evidence admission. Our working and client material is in state-of-the-art services, which are endangered 24/7 and reachable only to lawful staffs.

Market investigation can effortlessly be seen as the basis of advertising, so any advertising choice needs souk investigation sustenance, however simple or compound, to have the best chance of being seen definitely by your clienteles and rival.

With Infinit Date, we take on the vigorous but very dull task of meaningful what your clients want.

By partnering with Infinit Datum for subcontracted exploration facilities, your inner advertising side can attention more on

Business Invention

understandings, mature ground-breaking plans, and carry realizable deed plans. We help you learn more about your customers' needs and penchants and focus on production better occupational verdicts.

YOUTUBE CHANNEL

You can customary up a YouTube channel for your commercial by integration of all your videos. That way, you can tailor your station with descriptions that embody your corporation. Your channel comprises an info piece where you can offer a fleeting explanation of your professional and a relationship to your website or exchange specifics.

In your channel, you'll group the videos you've shaped and uploaded, the videos you've watched, and the playlists of the videos you've shaped.

Your channel has a web address (URL) that you can endorse on your website or advertising physical. People can subscribe to your channel. That is, when you sign in to YouTube, your videos seem on your YouTube homepage.

You can also make playlists on your YouTube channel to form your videos by subject or type. For example, you could have a playlist of videos for each of your creation categories, or a playlist of videos paid by your clienteles to a video competition you've run.

The Benefits of Using YouTube for Business

Using YouTube videos for commercial advertising drives is flattering gradually general with makes about the world. These makes instigated to appreciate that clienteles want to see more video satisfied from industries. You also documented the welfares of a YouTube channel.

1. It is a free platform

Would you give away a free chance to endorse your commercial if it goes out to be tremendously fruitful?

I'm good-looking sure you will not do it if repayment pays off.

Business Invention

Marketing for your corporate is not always free. It wants to venture in Google ads, common media ads, and all genera of ways to fetch your corporate to the world. And if you're a small occupational that does not have a big ROI yet, you only have an imperfect quantity of promotion prices. Providentially, there are ways to encourage your occupational that can accomplish remarkable fallouts without having to employ tons of change.

YouTube is a great stage for small industries to produce their product without disbursing for it.

Making a YouTube channel for your occupational is free, easy, and tremendously actual if you get it right. All you have to do is symbol up for a Google Account, and location up your YouTube channel is pretty forthright.

Contingent on the videos you create, you may need some devices such as a decent camera, a microphone, and a tripod. For editing, you'll find great video editing gears that are permitted and have the rudimentary topographies you prerequisite for novices. Consequently, you do not have to capitalize in an expert excision tool at the commencement.

Even though you prerequisite to employ a jiffy of your apparatus and devote time constructing content and encouraging your network, this is unimportant and dense speculation. Dissimilar impermanent content in social media, you'll construct a long-term, immortal, publicity channel. Afterward certain time, you can make money with your YouTube channel to upsurge your income.

2. It is an ever-growing platform

Where are you observing for rapid repairs for your glitches?

You do not distinguish how to accumulate your equipment? Need a lecture on cutting out pictures in Photoshop? Elaborate some inspiration for a petite enhancement?

Business Invention

I flutter you commonly (if not each time) go to YouTube. Arrive your exploration enquiry in the hunt block and there you take it. A lot of videos to resolve your glitches. So sort out a big portion of the residents. This conduct transported YouTube 1.58 billion manipulators by 2018.

"The amount of hours people devote viewing videos on YouTube has augmented 60% year-over-year, the wildest development we've realized in two years."

Persons are open-handed inspecting TV in courtesy of YouTube. Figures show that 6 in 10 individuals desire online video allotment to live TV.

Are you persuaded that YouTube is rising fast and progressively?

You also have admittance to people all over the place. This characterizes an occasion for your business to enlarge internationally.

By means of YouTube to endorse businesses disclosures your product to an emergent spectators that desire video content for entertainment and education. Your spectators are by now there, why not?

3. Just present your products

Clients believe commercial video content further than no matter what else. Since over videos they may be able to essentially see the yields in accomplishment and not just recite an explanation of them.

Video content is the utmost prevalent kind of content these days, and not just for the reason that of YouTube. Videos yield over the internet. For instance, videos on Facebook consume the broadest spread and uppermost commitment rates.

By representing the welfares of your merchandises or facilities over video content, your forecasts are further likely to faith your trade and convert to clients.

Do the auctions for your business occur on your website?

It's decent. By means of YouTube for your corporate does not mean that your spectators requests to be vended straight on YouTube's stage.

It's easy to get viewers to your site using action prompts from your YouTube videos. If you tell people your website in the video and tell them to check it out, they'll usually do what they're told.

Viewers who come to your website through your YouTube videos already know about you. You know who you are and what you have to offer. This makes them more open to buying your services or products.

4. Build awareness and credibility

How do persons turn out to be conscious of your product?

How can possible customers' belief in your business?

Furthermost company's emphasis on their website to acquire the work completed. Otherwise, practice social media podiums to upsurge brand consciousness and recover the dependability of their amenities. Though communal media is not ignored and should be a share of any company advertising policy to be efficacious, it's not the only permitted way to put your product in the attention.

Making a YouTube commercial page brands it easy for you to size trustworthiness for the services or products you offer. Not solitary do you use the YouTube Business Channel to display your foodstuffs and endorse your variety unswervingly. They also use it to kinda real assembly with possible forecasts.

YouTube stretches you the occasion to display how decent you are in your ground. You can impart persons services connected to your place, philanthropic them guidance and presentation them late the divisions of your profitable. With this happy, people knowledge what's late your brand.

Business Invention

Reason about it for an instant. You need to rent a business to aid your communal media podiums. Who would you rent? A corporation that you can deliver about on their website or a corporation that also has a YouTube channel that instructs persons on how to use communal media positively for industries? I believe that another will have a superior impression on your result since you have the indication that they distinguish what they are doing.

5. Gain customers with your expertise

Do you have actual information in your part? I consider you do it.

Why not portion this information with others to let them see that you are skilled in your position?

This offers you a countless benefit over your contestants, as you are professed as a noteworthy disposition in the ground. It will also benefit you to appeal to new patrons by showing that you are countless fit for the job.

Even if you suggest numerical facilities or are a native corporation, assemble a YouTube channel where you share the forte classified is another stage near rising your corporate. If you pick to be skilled, spectators will ask for your facilities.

Let's say you are an internal stylish. You twitch a YouTube channel where you give people instructions on how to pick the shades for their household, which properties to select for the living room, and how to make the kitchen more applied. Persons will watch your videos and be astonished by your knowledge. Some may reason, "She knows precisely what she's doing. Why don't you practice them to make my home in its place of doing a bad job yourself?".

Constructing a YouTube channel can make a big change in a minor commercial marketing strategy that works to attract the first customers. And can also help establish brands to expand their business.

If you'd like to extend your marketing strategy to YouTube, here's a guide that explains the steps to start a YouTube beginner channel.

Types of videos for your YouTube business channel

If you use YouTube for commercial advertising, you must choose which videos you upload to your YouTube channel. It's tremendously significant that you propose a YouTube content plan that aids your usual goals, get steady content, and quantity fallouts. I will direct you through the most lucrative kinds of video satisfied for productions.

1. Videos face to camera

When you display your look in the videos and look out your spectators speak, the assembly you usual up with spectators is more influential.

Face-to-Camera videos are the finest advertising technique on YouTube. They appeal the most courtesy since it feels more like a discussion than just a seminar video. Persons want to see faces and reply better to corporations that show their looks behind the screen.

If you look at the most effective businesses, you'll discover that there is insufficient real person complicated with the occupational.

Advertising via YouTube

2. Whiteboards

If you are not complete to display your look in obverse of the camera, do not be dispirited. You can still use a YouTube channel.

There are all kinds of filmed content kinds that you do not essential to film physically. One of the humblest and most attractive ways to instruct people deprived of a face-to-camera method is to use whiteboard simulation.

You perhaps saw them since they are very prevalent and produce a lot of appointment. They choose up the speech and syndicate it with an energetic design. The illustration shadows the story being verbal. This is a countless way to get a purer picture of the theme and to deliver graphic facts on more problematic themes.

3. Instructions and tutorials

Most people devote their period on YouTube to conversation and study things.

That's why how-to and seminar videos are tremendously current.

In the position you are in, you will assuredly bargain themes that you can use to update your spectators. Even video classes on by your products or amenities are a great idea.

Distillate on charitable your spectators some services connected to your facilities. This will support individuals see that you see the theme really well and upsurge the sureness they have in your profitable.

There are dissimilar types of classes. These can be face-to-face videos or you cannot display your expression. In some topics, you can make classes for screen sharing. If you're learning about using a software or app, all you have to do is shoot the awning and record your voice. Other themes let you to make performances.

It all depends on the themes. For instance, when you're collecting equipment, you'll need to record a seminar when collecting the furniture. You cannot just talk about it without viewing it.

4. Show your knowledge

It's your fortuitous to display people why they should faith your commercial.

Talk about your skills and what you erudite on the way. Show people how much you know about the subject and do not be frightened to share individual stories (deliberate them pertinent to the theme).

YouTube video advertising is even more actual when private stories are a portion of the satisfied policy. People incline to texture associated with a product and seriously believe their facilities if they can attach the commercial to an individual they price. However, this does not mean that you should start important stories about your dog (only if your function is animal related).

Talk about instructions and guidance that are applicable to your commercial.

Q & A videos are a countless way to part your information with your spectators. Spectators ask your enquiries and give them the responses they are observing for. These videos are more loquacious and individual than gratified of any kind, as they answer right to the watcher's needs.

5. Certificates

Testaments are influential since others promise for your knowledge. They display real people who were content with their facilities. If you can get some clienteles to test your facility, it will improve the apparent price of your commercial and bring you more clienteles.

If you are not a native corporation, getting video transfers from regulars can be tough. You can use Fiverr for that stock. You have a segment enthusiastic to the references in which you can rent actors. They obtain the real printed recommendations from real clienteles and can be recited by a performer in front of the camera. While it may complete alluring, I endorse that you do your finest to get in bit with real patrons. Your audiences will have a countless occasion when a performer buries your reliability.

There are convinced queries that you can ask your clienteles to get substantial references to reinforce your product. What was your key anxiety when purchasing our creation? Which topographies did you relish the most? Would you endorse this produce? The influence of the recommendations lies behindhand the enquiries asked.

6. No to sales talks

Do not reduce into the trick of continuously talking about your commercial. "No one enjoys to be sold, but everybody likes to purchase." - Frank Kern Keep this in attention when making satisfied for your channel.

Spectators will receive droplet off your videos directly if you admire your product universally. It's okay to part your brand's assets from time to time, but do not do everything about them. Using YouTube for occupational advertising is more than marketing as a top-store salable.

The main determination of introduction of a YouTube channel for your commercial is to attach with latent predictions that will finally develop your clienteles. The key here, however, is that you can only have faith in your product if you add worth to your lifespan through your happy.

Think of your YouTube frequency as another way to help your customs. They give people something valuable and they will recompense you by fetching clients and promoters of your sort.

Choose the right content for your channel

Now that you know what kinds of filmed satisfied you can generate for your YouTube channel, deliberate which ones are finest for your corporate.

Deliberate your aim spectators and what kind of content welfares you more.

Folks visit YouTube to talk or to discover answers to their problems. What problems do your viewers have concerning your place? How can you assist them to resolve these difficulties?

You also have to deliberate what your contestants are previously responsibility. You do not want to do precisely what others do, because then your product is not unusual. To distinguish physically, you have to bargain a diverse method. You can each advance the satisfaction of your entrants or correct the subjects from a changed outlook.

Be imaginative. The key to an effective YouTube channel is unique and faithful.

BUSINESS IDEA

A. INVESTMENT ADVISER:

Introduction

Let's look it, as a speculation consultant, you perhaps do not have period to set a complete advertising plan and start applying manifold schemes together with your present assignment. Once we appreciate that, we've clear to put a composed list of 8 rapid and original ways that you can souk yourself - definite to be stress-free. Without further ado, here they are:

1. Lunch and learning

Lunch and education are just what they complete like: eat while erudition. You can suggest these short meetings to businesses and businesses near your office. Just go there, give a 10-30 minute performance on a theme that your clienteles would usually like to overhear about, debate the amenities obtainable, and leave a commercial card. It does not take too much time for your day and gives people time to relish their lunch break.

2. Publish newsletters

Newsletters are super easy and countless if you like to inscribe. This is one of the many ways you can give worth and information to your clienteles. Envisage preliminary with a regular email highlighting what's new in your commercial, giving them information or replying often asked queries. From here, you can extra progress your newsletter and create it as difficult as you like. You may even add symbols.

3. Host a seminar or webinar

Sessions and webinars are alike in term and setting. They are together ways of accomplishment and calming the spectators, much like eating and knowledge. The only change between these two is that one individual is successively in person and the other connected. That's why you would not even have to leave your office if you do not want to. We endorse that a session or webinar takes about 30 to 45 minutes and shelter some precise features of a parental topic.

4. Contact journalists

Native newspapers are typically very content to handle some stimulating native actions or have a monetary skilled on pointer which can be called and referenced when desirable. Commerce some reporters and see what's up there. If you want to try your writing, you may be able to write a broadsheet or monthly fiscal dealings column. The really great thing about this promotion method is that it's free and besieged at persons who live close. This will give you more chances to find patrons that are applicable to your model souk.

5. Send tickets

Cards are actually nice, inexpensive and considerate. With the trips just around the angle, this is a mainly good period to try it out. If you are lime or paperless, e-cards are a countless choice. They are also free, which gives you the chance to refer more. Try transfer some singular cards for odd holidays, such as the Nationwide Sandwich Day, or mark them by transferring out a card during National Teacher's Day if one of your regulars transpires to be a teacher. For the lowest charge and exertion collection, just twig to gift and Christmas cards. This gives a predominantly nice touch and displays that you've taken care of physically without having to apply hours conniving some difficult maps for nationwide scrubbing your car day.

6. Talk to meetings

This method does not vary from that of dine and studies, with the only big change being the situation and the condition. In its place development a whole performance and establishing approximately that receipts more time, you should ask physically if you might make a short performance of about 5 minutes during a weekly conference in a business. You can even do this at some native club conferences in the city, such as: In sports or establishments. Get original and see if you cannot spread people who are not essentially on the detector in other circumstances.

7. Professional website

Of course, we resolutely trust in the influence of a specialized website here on Mentor websites. This is an inordinate way to smear a very contemporary publicity method. With your website, persons around the creation can find, meet and attach with you. If you essential tips on producing traffic and SEO experts, we endorse that you couple this whitepaper with your website.

8. Sponsor Youth Sport

If you're observing for a way to spread more clienteles in your part while giving approximately back to your local public, backing youth sporting is a countless way to do it! You can contribute some cash to the native sports team by adding your logo to their sweater or hitting a fence in the stadium. In this way, you develop a significant main nourishment in public and turn to the parentages of the offspring in the sports doings and attach with them by the presentation you the care.

B. HOUSE INSPECTOR

As the real plantation souk is on the up, it has never been a healthier time to get your home examination diploma. Customers are procurement and vending more frequently, and with more capitals endorsing a "buyer- caution" attitude, they do so with a new, careful viewpoint. The weakening of the souk in new years has led to indecision about home procurement. Clienteles and real plantation managers are intense to buy and sell families that assure that clienteles get what they pay for. House examiners are the key to safeguarding that clienteles are content with their acquiring choices. This means that there is an unbelievable chance to twitch and function a fruitful home examination commercial.

Preliminary a family examination commercial does not have to be a vision. Learn more about linking our team.

If you are attentive in opening your own home examination occupational, here are some key advice to help you prosper in the manufacturing:

To be insured

The home examination commerce is exclusive in that there is no business average for guarantee. Inappropriately that incomes that there are many examiners who work without assurance. The house examination insurance confirms that you and your client are financially secure if you are exposed to unforeseen circumstances. Customers are counseled to rent a house examiner who transmits insurance. That's why it's a vigorous part of your business.

Provide reports

The examinations will not be accomplished on a circumstance by case basis. House examiners should offer their clienteles with a comprehensive crash specifying the disorder of all machineries of their home. In many cases, homebuyers need this examination crash to gain home assurance or full backing support.

Picture yourself

Your house examination credential gives you the information you need for safe and detailed reviews, but there is much more to learn. As a home checker, you also want to study more about real plantation performs, structure codes and present building trends. Take every chance to speak with others in the industry, join classes and contribute in shops. Your information will be a real tool to build a solid client base for your home review commercial.

Create a business network

Your corporation is going to examine much more than just from home. That's why it's authoritative to construct a solid system of persons who can help you flourish in promotion, purchaser facility, secretarial, expansion, and journalism. You also want to join events where you can build associations with real plantation agents, potential purchasers, and workers so that people reminisce your name when it's time to have their home examined.

Building your own home examination commercial can be easier if you capitalize on a low-cost permit with A Purchaser's Choice. Not only do we offer the tools you need to become a superintendent for your home, we'll help you select an assurance corporation, we'll deliver you with a journalism instrument that will make your rumors quick, easy and useful, and deliver training chances in numerous areas. In terms of home examination, we can deal a system of well-known, knowledgeable home examination specialists who can support you every phase of the way.

Develop marketing materials

Every specialized business needs high-class occupational postcards, marks, flyers, banners, and clothing. Our mate, BlueWater Commercial Upgrades, confirms that the examiners of ABCHI have skillfully calculated advertising factual. This is in link with our marking, which is reproduced on high excellence supplies using up-to-date finishing methods. BlueWater reproduction is a full-service facility that necessitates the assumption of project and lithography of the industry's foremost advertising supplies.

C. INSURANCE BROKER

Protection mediators are accountable for classifying and establishing suitable assurance attention for profitable administrations and persons.

Insurance brokers work organized between clienteles and assurance corporations and find the best assurance treatment for the purchaser.

The errands of the career differ conferring to the size and type of company: Smaller businesses bargain fewer occasions for specialism than larger corporations. They could effort in trade assurance and overall attention in parts such as property, travel, motor vehicle and animal assurance or profitable assurance, which contract with more multifaceted, high-value areas such as delivery, flying and oil and gas.

Here are 7 marketing ideas for insurance agents:

1. Implement Content Marketing

As an assurance agent, your clienteles are in the forefront, which just wants an assurance strategy. However, you must also emphasize on possession in a bit with patrons during the months and years between these contacts. For patrons in this point of their breaths, it is not applicable that you accept charities to insurance needs. In its place, share contents that comprise appreciated information that is suitable for clienteles irrespective of the place of the assurance procedure. That way you visit in the head so they will reminisce you when it matters.

2. Hug social media

Most use social media, but do you use these networks as an assurance manager to produce and endorse your occupational? If you say no, brand it your board for 2018. When you think about where clienteles and forecasts are, you can bargain them online.

One error that assurance negotiators make with community media is just "boring" assurance evidence. Get imaginative and share content diagonally to all your pages that are attractive and appreciated, whether or not they are presently in the souk for a strategy. Ask motivating inquiries, ask your system and comprise your own feelings in the explanations. This is another way to attach with your clients and predictions who are amusing and not observing for work.

3. Monitor your online reviews

Customers have the chance to recover or breakdown the standing of your business through places such as Google Reviews, Yelp, and Facebook Assessments. In detail, 97 percent of customers read online appraisals for local industries in 2017, and 85 percent of patrons trust online appraisals as well as a private endorsement. With such proportions, it's vital to accept these online appraisals, which should be added to your business doings for 2018.

Are you doubting how to do that? The quick reply is to do a decent job and have content clienteles who want to crow about you. Clienteles may not know how valued these appraisals are for you. Consequently, it is significant to take the time to ask for these appraisals. If you need help situation up your online appraisals, we've put composed 10 tips.

To accomplish your online vertical, you must display the websites and be practical. The aptitude to give a confident rating also means that a buyer can leave an undesirable rating. Negative appraisals are best fingered by following, asking questions, and finding out how to better achieve the condition in the forthcoming. Recollect, you cannot make every client 100% content, and that's fine. Do your best work and deliver brilliant client service. Your faithful purchaser base will produce and your confident evaluations will be.

4. Ensuring brand consistency

This means having a united product in all online and offline networks. What this does not mean is uploading a symbol or a headshot to any website that may be applicable to your corporate and never revenues. You need to make sure your info is the same on every network - on your website, on websites and on communal media shapes, and so on - and then vigorously display it.

In adding to material and descriptions, the involvement of a scene or customer should be dependable across each channel. Answer to mails, tweets, emails, and phone calls in the same tenor and share the same evidence. The involvement of each purchaser or view should be the same notwithstanding of when, where, or how he finds you.

You never want to slip a shopper because they called the wrong number or directed a message to the wrong email. Evade this by taking the time obligatory to preserve a dependable product.

5. Go mobile

Do you know where your telephone is? Like most individuals these days, it's within spread. Mobile practice endures to produce as users devote over 5 hours a day on their mobile strategies. To attend the mounting mobile spectators, you should emphasize on a receptive website so that users staying via a mobile phone or tablet have as much knowledge as operators with a desktop computer.

And there are many internet users on their phones. Internet users devote 51 percent of their period on mobile devices or tablets, while desktop workers devote 48 percent of their period. Facebook is the most broadly secondhand social media podium in the biosphere, with 1.149 billion users using mobile only. These are many latent patrons! Evade difficulties with patrons and predictions, and attention on educating your mobile involvement this year.

6. Do not wait, clean up your data

If you have a folder of bad associates, all the exertion to make and send newsletters is misused. If you take too many recoils, unsubscriptions, or junk reports, your dispatcher's status and your aptitude to even send it to the inbox will also fall abruptly.

Clean data move your email deliverability and your aptitude to surge your reach. Take the time to sometimes clean up your data and eradicate unsubscribe requirements to make sure you get the most from your promotion pains.

7. Automate your marketing

As an assurance agent, dealing a strong cylinder of consumers and scenarios is serious to mounting your corporate. You have a long list of errands that you do on a daily, weekly, monthly, and yearly basis. That means it can be hard to find time to produce satisfied and share it with earlier patrons.

Mechanical e-mail and social media selling is a great way to spread your mark spectators enduringly, even if you do not have time to choice up the phone or send the handwritten note. There are numerous gears that you can use to mechanize this yourself. But if you want to create comfortability for you from launch to end, automatic advertising on the Outbound Machine is the right optimal for your commercial.

D. MORTGAGE BROKERS

Remortgage agent promotion is usually nobody that you would find advanced. It is based on outdated promotion methods and is often not very communicating. With promotion mechanization, mortgage brokers can generate mechanical messages built on distinct purchaser needs and response to instrument remortgage advertising thoughts. Let's look at a few ideas that include attractive customers and cumulative faithfulness while dipping assignment.

1) Use social media to your benefit. If you are not lively on social media, you will slip the occasion to attach with new latent patrons. Social media is a great way to vitrine your information as a remortgage broker, attach with other businesses in the public, build product mindfulness, answer procurer queries, and more. Use automatic social media organization to get the most out of your period and admission low-cost loan requests.

2) You must distinguish your remortgage brokerage amenities from the throng and surge the auctions of your loan brokers. One way to take confident consideration to your professional and charm new clients is to get transfers. Ask for a transfer after every client you help. You can do this effortlessly through humble online surveys. With an all-in-one

Business Invention

advertising resolution for hypothecation brokers, you can easily produce and issue studies. You will not get an endorsement from every client, but you will get some useful response to progress your amenities.

3) Arrest your online leads in feature so you can interact with them for myself. Even if a interaction comes to your website and the interaction particulars are not left, you can still pleat much evidence about it. Lead following tracks a tip, roads where they come from, archives, which relatives they click, and so on. This will generate a comprehensive private shape for each principal. When the lead shrubberies its email or phone number, you can reach it. By continually gathering online data, you can discover which areas of your site obtain the most courtesy, so you can enhance the site.

With individual outlines, you can also attach to clues grounded on their separate welfares and online actions.

4) Chat live with patrons and tips straight on your website. A conscious chat tool is priceless as it offers a way to attach straight with online companies in its place of vocation and to come on the phone. While glancing your website, live chat is always obtainable on the shade. They are there to respond to queries or opinion in the right course.

5) Make modified remortgage broker movements for each of your customers. With advertising mechanization, emails can be mechanically sent to each purchaser, giving to their own needs and partialities. This helps you construct devotion and buyer loyalty, but you do not have to employ extra time fashioning operations. Just select how your mails should be sent, and they will be referred to your patrons in due course.

E. PLUMBING COMPANY

The hygiene commercial is a vital commercial as clienteles and industries are usually incapable of preserving their own cleanliness schemes. Installers confirm that consumption aquatic and sewer pipes

Business Invention

are correctly upheld and obey with local structure codes. Clienteles usually live in inhabited real plantation. However, some installers accept business or salable agreements and effort solely with corporations.

For whom is this business suitable?

This corporate is a model for folks who like to exertion with their indicators, are not frightened to get dirty, and have supple working hours. Some installers are called to a building site in a spare then have to work late or even at the vacation. Plumbers and a sanitation corporation may also need to work on public outings.

What happens on a typical day in a plumbing business?

The day-to-day doings of a plumber comprise rereading purchaser records, fixing and preserving sanitation tackle, and billing purchaser services. Some corporations also apply a lot of time scheming and structure new sanitation organizations when salaried on new edifice projects.

Installers also apply a lot of time accumulating pipe sections, piping, and fixtures using immobilizers, screws, bolts, cement, plastic solvents, and caulking, fusing and joining guns, connections and welding equipment.

Installers also normally have to make composite cunnings on structure sites that govern the fortification and permanency of the penetrating they plan, install, and keep.

What is the target market?

Customers are typically profitable clienteles or secluded patrons. Installers typically obtain deals either through transfers or through embattled advertising such as direct mail. The coolest way for plumbers to do occupational is to acquire a sending list from people who have before done sanitation or sanitation work with plumbers in the last 6 months to a year. Then email these people with an offer for promotion amenities.

How does a plumbing business make money?

Sanitation corporations responsibility a bump sum (sometimes plus material) for jobs. However, you can also compute hourly or best additions for spare, rush, or off-hour facilities.

What is the growth potential of a plumbing company?

A sanitation commercial can typically be ongoing with a plumber. As request begins to surpass the plumber's aptitude, extra plumbers can be lent as employees or as sovereign workers. Most plumbers uphold a local custom, although some have accomplished to increase their occupational beyond their district.

What are the steps to start a sanitary company?

When you're ready to start your hygiene commercial, follow these ladders to make sure your occupational is law-abiding, and save time and cash as your corporate grows:

1. Strategy your commercial. A clear plan is critical to the achievement of a businessperson. A few significant issues to deliberate are your early cost, your target souk, and how long it takes to reach breakeven.

2. Form a lawful thing. The formation of a permissible thing avoids you from being for myself answerable if your salubrious firm is prosecuted.

3. List for duties. You need to list for a diversity of central and central taxes before you can sign up for an occupational.

4. Open a corporate interpretation. A keen checking interpretation for your sanitation corporate keeps your assets in order and makes your corporate appear more qualified.

5. Set up Commercial Secretarial. Taking your numerous expenditure and income brooks are dangerous to empathetic the monetary act of your corporate. Keeping correct and comprehensive accounts will greatly streamline your yearly tax return.

6. Gain the obligatory documents and certificates. Disappointment to get the essential licenses and certificates can consequence in heavy penalties or even the end of your commercial.

7. Get a profitable cover. The assurance is strongly suggested to all occupational proprietors. If you rent workers, the employee recompense assurance may be obligatory by law in your nation.

8. Outline your make. Your product is what your commercial attitudes for and how you're commercial is professed by the civic. A strong product helps your occupational stand out from the struggle.

9. Set up a web occurrence. Through a business website, clienteles can teach more about your business and the products or facilities you suggest. You can also use communal media to entice new customers or customers. Save 15% when generating a commercial website with Weebly.

How to promote and market a plumber business

Publicity of your plumber's commercial typically needs a multi-faceted method when you first start. If you before worked as an apprentice, you may have beforehand made acquaintances in the manufacturing. You are not allowable to take your previous company's patrons with you, but you can inspire new patrons to do a commercial with you, based on the standing of your old boss and the fact that you have operated under a plumber craftsman.

Direct mail is another way to do commercial. By buying a mailing list of persons and businesses that have before paid for sanitation work, you can tap into a board souk for your amenities. Send them an offer to familiarize them to your new drainage system company.

Lastly, ask friends and personal for transfers to build a patron base.

How can the customers come back?

Become known in your manufacturing for something. For instance, can you be the first installer in your area who promises to arrive on time and spotless up after concluding work? Clean companies have a bad standing since they are late, late, and have poor purchaser service. Be the other firm.

You can also specify. Become a plumber who works wholly with exact types of companies. Get to know their sole needs and funds. Take care of them and they will never want to do occupational again with a "general plumber."

F. ELECTRICIAN COMPANY

Electrician corporation's emphasize mainly on the upkeep of electrical schemes in backgrounds and productions. Since it is an exchange corporation, it is highly particular. In adding, local and state administrations typically limit non-manual labors to work on electrical schemes. These issues usually necessitate fit electricians.

For whom is this business suitable?

This commercial is intended for people who are good with their pointers, have good human skills and can resolve multifaceted theoretical and motorized glitches and work in a diversity of different surroundings. To own and work as an electrician, you must also be a skilled electrician. Most businesspersons are electricians who have been trained as learners for many years.

What happens on a typical day as an electrician?

Business Invention

The daily doings of an electrician comprise mending or substituting electrical schemes, including main systems, fuse and switch box panels, steering electrical cables, revamping and servicing electrical cables, modifiers, and related systems. Electricians also employ a lot of time answering electrical snags.

Because cabling in a home or commercial is often concealed behind walls, electricians need to know how to identify them before a scheme can be mended. You may not have the treat of pull to pieces all the fortifications of construction to solve the problem.

What is the target market?

Electricians make cash by accusing clienteles for their facilities. You can charge hourly fees or custody a flat fee for facilities.

How does an electrician make cash?

Favorite types of patrons for this occupational are interchange financial records. However, private patrons can also be an endless source of income, provided that the company can serve a circling purchaser base. This could embrace an agreement with a homeowner reminder or other planned municipal to serve suburban customers.

What is the growth potential for an electrician?

Most electricians are run as owner/operative businesses. However, you can take on a trainee or work with many dissimilar associates and build an advanced volume commercial. Some electricians are also run as permits. If you go this way, you should be ready to pay a considerable quantity in the loan. However, permit businesses offer some great welfares, such as: B. a recognized product name, endangered provision areas, and continuing promotion support.

What are the costs of opening an electrician business?

The cost of a preliminary electrician occupational varies, but normally comprises licensing, cover, union fees, overhead and gear costs, and hire charge for office space. In over-all, many startup companies dedicate at least $ 5,000 on entry. These costs do not include the education or training time, which can range from $ 3,000 to $ 20,000, liable on whether you choose a public college, a practical school, or a secluded university.

What are the steps to start an electrician business?

When you're ready to start your electrician's profitable, follow the ladders below to make sure your commercial is honest, and save time and cash as your commercial grows:

1. Plan you're occupational. A clear plan is critical to the accomplishment of a businessperson. A few significant issues to reflect are your first cost, your target market, and how long it takes to reach breakeven.

2. Form a legal object. The creation of a legal unit avoids you from being for myself responsible if your electrician is sued.

3. List for taxes. You need to list for a diversity of central and centralized tolls before you can sign up for a corporate.

4. Open a commercial account. An enthusiastic examination explanation for your electrician keeps your monies in instruction and makes your occupational appear more specialized to your patrons.

5. Set up Business Secretarial. Taking your various expenditure and proceeds streams is critical to sympathetic the monetary recital of your business. Keeping correct and thorough the books will greatly streamline your annual tax return.

6. Get the compulsory licenses and authorizations. Disappointment to get the required documents and authorizations can outcome in heavy punishments or even the finish of your corporate.

7. Get a commercial cover. The cover is powerfully optional to all commercial proprietors. If you rent operates, the worker recompense cover may be obligatory by law in your country.

8. Define your product. Your make is what your occupational opinions for and how you're occupational is supposed by the public. A strong brand helps your professional stand out from the struggle.

9. Set up web attendance. Through a commercial website, clienteles can learn more about your occupational and the foodstuffs or amenities you offer. You can also use social media to fascinate new patrons or patrons. Save 15% when producing a professional website with Weebly.

G. PAINTING

Company Introduction

A canvas occupational is a great way to make money, it's climbable and it's not as hard as you think to outstrip the struggle.

How to start a canvas commercial

Register your company

The careful type of registering you need for your commercial can diverge by state. Therefore, it is a good idea to visit your administration website or some local skill governments to find out precisely what is wanted. From there, you can also acquire assurance, field, and holding for your occupational website.

Invest in equipment

Apart from that, the only real startup prices your commercial must have are the gear. You may need rankings, salvers, encounters, breakers, needles, covers, and perhaps cars with your business's logo to do numerous errands.

Find worthy partners

When it comes to finding regulars, Lewis mentions verdict the other concerns in your area that have the most influence on your target customers.

He explains, "It's important that you create a top 100 list of influencers in your community to generate referrals. You should consider whether you are targeting estate agents, commercial real estate managers, and other B2B service companies such as roofers, gutter installers, and floor publishers. Limit your list to 100 and live with them via email, email, text, social media, and personal visits or networks. Keep a hard-core buy-or-die philosophy. "

Create your conversation points

You also need to think about what your marketing materials and sales talk should embrace in happy. Why should a new purchaser take your corporation from the other options existing?

Lewis says, "Build an analytical auctions course that purposes to instruct clients about how your canvas corporate changes from the distinctive painter firm. Agreements, assurances, patron reviews, and artist airing progressions should come first in your messaging so that the buyer can know how to lessen risk and make more value in taking your business. "

Follow the perspectives

However, charming new clienteles is not as easy as a distribution sales pitch with some important influencers. You need to go ahead and stay in justly continuous communication.

Lewis says, "Use strong pre-positioning, performance, post-positioning, and follow-up tactics that reproduce client anxieties and the sales cycle. Keep in mind that dye services are classy and can often take months to make a acquisitions conclusion. Hold on."

Set clear rates

Concerning your tariffs, Lewis says you need to classify three key influences in advance: manufacture rates, salary rates, and fees. The making rate would be the time it takes a regular painter to paint a specific shallow. Pay charges are what you pay your staffs. And the fee rates are what a client is actually exciting for an hour's work.

Lewis adds, "When you evaluate a project, your only job is to degree the right-angled, the undeviating material, and the number of faces or objects you draw. After that, it's just a math badly-behaved of the fourth grade. Never a flashing guesstimate. Always use your pricelists and formulas. "

Study the business concepts

In addition, Lewis adds that many house artistes are more absorbed on the artiste lateral of their profitable than on the actual profitable landscapes of clerical and publicity. However, it is a good idea to have these ideas under switch as well.

Lewis says, "Most of the paint worker trades are authorities who have arrived the world of free enterprise. Few have ever taken the time to be a grave student at the commercial end of their business. I urge all proprietors to take jobs in their careers to involve in advertising, sales, processes and organization. Doing this for a short, strong time pays off for your life! "

Build a portfolio

Working with customers can also be a great way to photo and record your work, giving you examples of future forecasts and predictions. This can show the excellence of your work and prove that you have a large number of content patrons.

Stay in touch with customers

If you have operated with a number of clients, do not trust that these clienteles will come back to you to meet all their image needs.

Lewis explains, "The major error I see in paint businesses is charitable up and abandoning customers after the sale. As an outcome, the sales costs go through the roof and force the servicer to erratic starvation cycles. When I work with an artiste firm that's stuck in terms of sales and success, that's typically the main reason for their letdown."

Invest in marketing

You can also participate in some online advertising actions such as email newsletters, retargeting ads, and local SEO to entice both new and old customers.

Lewis says, "For well-known workers, I endorse patrons who want to reactivate patrons and used monthly email newsletters for stowage. Local SEO advertising can also be real, liable on your market and how much you are keen to participate."

H. HOME FOOD

For the individual who likes to cook or bake, it's a great way to syndicate a pastime with a vocation. As with other trades, a grocery store at home needs a lot of investigation and preparation to get started. However, you need extra permits, inspections, and advertising plans before you can make a sale. Here are some things to keep in mind when initial food occupational from home.

Choose your niche

Choose what kind of food you want to sell and how. A change of food-related commercial choices comprises catering, food delivery, and baked goods. You can emphasis on exact place markets, such as: Cookery weddings, food delivery for new moms or baked belongings sold in indigenous cafes or shops.

Conduct market research

It is very significant that you do your investigation before you start your grocery at home because the food manufacturing is very modest. Visit commercial schmoosing events such as the Small Business Growth Centers, SCORE and your local Cavities of Trade. This provides a great chance to pick the heads of local commercial people in food manufacturing and see what works and what does not.

Clippy McKenna, Creator of Food Ingredient Builder Clippy, says if you cannot demeanor more in-depth souk research, use your groups and the people you know to test your food recipes. Any comment you can get is cooperative.

Prepare a business plan

While a commercial plan does not have to be extra official, it does help you to grow an unclear idea for your grocery store at home and to make a more tangible plan for its application. If you need monetary support, you need to persuade your depositors of your general commercial policy and monetary outlook. If you need help generating a commercial plan, you can use the US Small Business Management Web site or work with SCORE, a net of employed and superannuated managers who share their know-how.

Licenses and permits

You must appraisal the local zoning rules to safeguard you are allowable to work a food corporate outside your home. Then, you may need to rent expert kitchen spaces. Next, you need to make sure your cooking gear meets all the food cleanliness necessities. Check with your national for more details.

In general, this means guaranteeing that your commercial kitchenette is clearly unglued from your individual kitchenette and that you are not using the gears in your expert kitchen for individual use. Take government-required food-handling courses to better comprehend all supplies. Finally, you want to get a commercial authorization and a resale certificate that allows you to buy tax-free elements.

Buy your equipment

Buy your tackle and components for food business from providers such as kaTom restaurant Stock, INC. Or General Hotel & Restaurant Supply. This depends on the type of food you can cook, but also comprises items such as bowls, casserole dishes, blenders, spoons, and other gears, as well as dimension matters. These, like the food fixings, should be kept distinct from your personal possessions. When you sell your goods through shops, you buy wrapping material to wrap your food.

If your state has category necessities, use a computer to create element tags for your food packing. For more info, contact your state's Section of Health. If you work as a caterer, you buy trays, bowls, and other substances that are good for public events.

Promote your business

Practice the group of groups you tried with your food and tutors when you came to your professional schmoozing events. According to Erin Fuller, Handling Director of the National Connotation of Women's Business Owners, she was able to gain her first client. According to Stephen Hall, writer of From Kitchen to Souk, you should hand out free examples of your food at native fairs and agriculturalists markets.

Also, contemplate using social media podiums like Facebook and Instagram or an e-commerce corporate with a stand like Shopify. Take many photos of your merchandises and probably add guidelines that use your food. In the end, be ready to vote unswervingly for superstores and emphasis groups. You want to see that you have an absorbed plan and plan for how your food fits on the shelf space.

I. CLEANING COMPANY

Business Invention

If you've already unlocked your housework commercial and bought your home cleaning assurance, you've taken a big step onward, and that merits a big thumbs up. But now you might be doubting how to make your commercial an achievement in the industry. Your latent clienteles have many home domestics to choose from, so you can discriminate your corporate from others! Here are some tips to help you rally your cleaning business.

1. Offer a personalized service and fair prices

Take some time to give free approximations. That way, you can see a latent client's home to see how much time it takes to clean it. Do not care the same price for a big house and for a small bed-sitter. Clienteles will go to a domestic they trust offers a fair deal. Sit down with the client to find out what he needs. According to studies, client involvement in a commercial has a big impression on the probability of periodic customers. This also put on to you. When you are with your clients to know what is important to them, you will take this bespoke deal and show that you take care of them and their needs, so that you can advance an assessing plan that is fair to you and yours It's worth it. And if you need to raise your prices? You will know sooner.

2. Manage your time carefully

To be fruitful, you need to refill your agenda. Working on your time organization will advantage both you and the purchaser as the prospects are clear and in line with authenticity. Plan your jobs so that you can modify more than one job per day. Slot machineries starting at 10am will not have sufficient time for an evening customer. But if you start at 8 in the pre-lunch, you can finish by noon and then go to extra customer - or even free up the much-needed time. It also means that your patron does not have to be locked out all day. Always be on time and well-organized to meet your diary and satisfy your clienteles.

3. Find your niche

Business Invention

In a packed market, getting a seat can be hard. Check online scores and social media to see what clienteles want and what the rivalry proposals. Then make a place. Maybe you have assurance that all your foodstuffs are ecologically welcoming. You may be able to offer supple agendas, such as: B. for the eras of time in the evening or on stays. Maybe you're working on a broadsheet newsletter or blog posts with free housework tips, outlines to your housework staff, and product reviews more about advertising. With a niche, you have a sole place in the market.

4. Use quality products

First of all, while low-cost crops save cash, using more luxurious quality crops will help you gain a sole custom that welfares your commercial in the extended term. The use of non-toxic and ecologically welcoming crops is better for the equipment and leaves no worrying vapors or odors in the home. These safe and healthy replacements are better for both your cleaner and the purchaser. Learn about new products through dealers, trade books, or industry relations to stay up to date.

5. Treat your employees well

Your staffs are the key to the accomplishment of your business. To provide unresolved spring-cleaning facility, you need to entice the best and most expert cleaning staff. Some ways to hearten your staffs to stay with you include:

- Spend time training; Show them how to clean spaces, clean a basin and more
- No micromanagement - show sureness and admiration as you train them
- Welfares such as paid sick leave or worker leave have shown that they show their faithfulness
- Offer plusses for excellence work

6. Spend time with marketing

Do not become self-assured if you have a dense client base. You need to devote time advertising to make sure you always have new clienteles. There are many ways to endorse your commercial in the right marketplaces. These include:

- Schmoosing - schmoozing does not cost cash in loan, but can lead to direct business chances? Let people know what you are doing.
- Interaction Real Estate Agents or Manufacturers - Contact businesses that may refer you to others. This means that you have already left the rivalry with a possible client, even before he is home.
- Promote Communal - This is a great way to find resident jobs. Make flyers, pay for ads in local fliers or publications, and get to know local communal events. This helps you to build variety alertness.

7. Focus on the business aspect

Structure of a positive home cleaning business is not easy, either in terms of housework itself or in terms of commercial organization. Trades need to be jobwise achieved to prosper. So that your home housework corporation can grow and enlarge, you do not just have to worry about housework. Make sure that you have a commercial plan, that you succumb taxes as needed, and that you have the cover you need to grow and prosper.

J. Book Keeping Consultation:

A secretarial commercial contains handling income and spending, processing payroll secretarial and making commercial tax returns. Generating a commercial plan and knowledge how to win clienteles are some instances of what you need to do to get started. If bookkeeping is just one way to make a little more money, you may be able to skip some ladders. We will point out these areas where suitable.

1. Become a certified accountant

One of the wildest ways to gain trustworthiness with possible clienteles is to prove that you have the secretarial annals you need. If you are a CPA, you have already confirmed that you have the data and skills to achieve the duties of a bookkeeper, and you can move on to another step.

However, if you have either official training in secretarial / office or have worked as a bookkeeper, you should gain documentation before starting a secretarial fixed.

There are two first-class specialized bookkeeper administrations for which you endorse warranty:

- American Organization of Expert Bookkeepers (AIPB) - To become AIPB certified, you must complete the 3,000-hour expert knowledge and pass a warranty exam. After guarantee, you will be given the right to put the letters CB (Certified Bookkeeper) behind your name and present it on your CV and professional cards, giving you a lead over bosses and latent clients. This documentation is idyllic if you have no proper education in accounting and secretarial.
- National Connotation of Expert Public Bookkeepers (NACPB) - To get NACPB guarantee, you must pass an examination and deliver indication that you have earned a subordinate or bachelor's degree in secretarial.
  Once you have the conventional assurance, you will receive the CPB (Certified Professional Bookkeeper). You can put these literatures in your CV, business cards, and other resources behindhand your name to show your presentation to bosses and future clienteles.
  Not only should you become an expert bookkeeper, but you should also reflect guarantee from some of the foremost secretarial software sellers, such as QuickBooks and

FreshBooks. For more info about how software guarantees work, see our Bookkeeper Certification Guide.

2. Create a business plan

Unless this is just a part-time entrance for you, you should write an occupational plan before you start the professional. While a corporate plan can positively be used to raise capitals for your professional, the value of lettering a corporate plan is all about the procedure.

While script a commercial plan, you can think about each feature of your commercial, counting what crops and facilities you sell, how you souk those crops and facilities, and who your rivalry is. You also make a monetary plan that should include a 12-month earnings and loss forecast, the expected cash flow, and a deliberate equilibrium sheet.

Here are the key points that should be included in each business plan:

- Location
- Precipitate
- Business impression
- Economical Inquiry
- Advertising Proposal
- Start-up charges
- Financial projections

3. Integrate your accounting business

As with starting a commercial, there are numerous managerial errands that must also be done before you can begin client service. This step is significant because it founds your business as genuine. It also helps to boundary your personal obligation. If your business is ever sued, you can only take corporate assets and not your personal properties, such as your home or private bank accounts. Whether you are working part-time or full-time, you do not want to skip this step.

Here is a specification of what you need to do to begin your commercial at the local, state, and central levels:

Select a business name

Naming your commercial can be a fun and wearing workout. Your name needs to take your product, as this looks like a latent client before connecting you for an initial conversation. You want to make sure your business name says precisely what you are doing so people will not have to deduction. This is not the time to be "sugary," unless you can also "elucidate" what you are doing at the same time.

Here are some great tips from commercial proprietors on how to name your occupational:

- Struggle for clearness - your name must tell persons what you do.
- Use a term with a well-known product - for example, you could use the name of the city you're in, as Stacey Giuliani did for his Lauderdale Comics (Fort Lauderdale) store.
- Get posts from others - ask domestic and networks for their effort; Have fun and show on your communal systems that you are looking for offers on how to name your corporate. Offer the champion a prize.
- Test it - Test possible patrons to see what they think. Compare your name with contestants' names to see if it attitudes out enough (but not too much).

Select a business structure

There are four common commercial constructions: sole proprietorship, business, imperfect accountability corporation (LLC) and firm. The assembly you choose regulates your own accountability, if the firm is ever sued, your tax responsibility and your capacity to elevation investment.

Business Invention

To help you make that choice, I inspire you to acquaint yourself with the four common occupational assemblies by understanding our Best Small Business Building Guide. Second, I extol that you interact with an attorney who can assess your state of affairs and help you make the right conclusion.

LawTrades will rent you with a devoted attorney who can contribution you in registration your commercial, choosing the right business construction, and smearing for a federal tax ID number and country ID number when signing staffs.

4. Set up business operations for your accounting business

Now that you've combined your commercial, you can start setting up procedures, such as: It's vital to distinct your commercial from your individual money in instruction to take full gain of the liability defense you obtain during the start-up course.

Set up a commercial bank account

One of the most dominant things you can do is distinct your commercial funds from your individual money. While most people think they should wait for the corporation to start making cash flow, I would not decide with that. It's much easier now to set up a commercial inspection explanation before the cash starts.

Another benefit of unravelling individual and commercial capitals is that the status of incomplete liability is reinforced. By combining your commercial and individual expenditure, you can lose the defense of your individual funds, as there is no way to discriminate between occupational and individual commercial.

K. BUSINESS CONSULTANT:

Many put-upon businesspersons and busy persons need to solve glitches that require know-how. Then they are looking for an expert consultant who will provide the information and gen they are absent for as long as they need help.

Starting self-governing referring rehearsal is one of the best ways to turn your information and years of involvement into a commercial. An advisor is an expert who advises others in a specific area or solves certain glitches. In an effort to improve consequences in their lives or in their commercial, people are asking one or more advisors to assess issues, provide solutions, and assist in implementing required changes.

Referring is dissimilar from training, which is another way to help others with their know-how. Psychotherapy classically attentions on corporations or groups as clients, although those sometimes seek mentors. Mentors judge an unruly and prepare a solution that focuses on progressions. In most cases, the work of the adviser is done after amplification and sustenance in the application of the key.

On the other hand, training is more often done as a one-to-one meeting, with an attention on construction a client's private fortes. Similar to psychotherapy, a teacher is usually involved (ie weekly) over an old-fashioned of time until the client has reached his goals.

While you can turn any kind of information into a referring firm, here are some of the best trades to deliberate.

1. Career Counselor

As the budget decelerates, the need for job psychotherapy grows. But even in good parsimonies, many people, from recent college old pupils to baby boomers looking for a new career in superannuation, can assistance from a job specialist.

A career therapist does many things, counting measuring client needs, preparing CVs, cover letters and other job-related leaflets, questioning job meetings, finding job support, endorsing exercise, and more.

The regular salary for a career therapist, according to Glassdoor, is $ 40,000.

However, this is envisioned for a job, as opposed to a self-employed adviser.

Often you can earn more on your own than in a job.

2. Leadership / Team Building Consultant

In the end, businesses are in the midpoint of care and want staffs who are well-organized and who work composed for the advantage of the commercial. However, many businesses have rules and staffs that affect output.

A management and team structure advisor works with an organization to deliver them with skills that stimulate those employed under them, counting problem-solving and policymaking skills, structure trust and relations, making a supportive work situation, and more.

3. Marketing consultant

Advertising is the key to commercial achievement. But many businesses, particularly secluded and small trades, often have no contextual in auctions and publicity or have no understanding of attention, to get people to entice and buy courtesy.

An advertising advisor measures a business's current advertising plan and plans, and then makes endorsements on how to advance results with more real messages and / or methods.

Income as an advertising advisor may vary contingent on the company you work with. Payscale intelligences that the regular early income for advertising advisers is $ 58,828.

4. Organizational / efficiency consultant

Business Invention

When time is money, inept use of time means progressive money. Based on this awareness, many corporations hire advisors to calculate how the business is working to recover its efficiency and competence.

Some things they look at comprise obtainable capitals and how well they are being used, how the body is organized, and how best to exploit the skills and involvements of the people complicated in the group.

The regular pay of a group advisor is $ 88,763.

5. Other types of advice

The selections registered in the preceding units focus on commercial referring, as it offers the most chances and the best revenue. However, there are many other types of information. In fact, many persons rent therapists to help them with their daily lives. Here is a list of some other types of guidance that you can reflect:

- Green Alive Referring
- Fitness and wellness guidance
- departure plans and private business advice
- Private Society and Efficacy (Rather than looking for a business, help individuals be organized, efficient, and productive)
- Business Economics / Accounting Consultancy
- Image referring
- Stress administration guidance

6.   Design your own career as a consultant

The fact is that there are many dissimilar sorts of therapy performs and the probability that somebody out there needs your information or desire, which can main to a checking firm.

Make a list of what you are good at. Are you a common employee with wedding or teaching? Reflect starting a association or childrearing business.

Business Invention

Can you buy food for a week for a few dollars? Start a coupon or a frugal housing discussion.

If you know your services and know how to use them to help others, then you should do marketplace investigation to see if there are persons eager to pay you for your information.

In addition, you can turn your know-how into incomes, counting training, blogging, info crops such as e-books, written articles, published videos, lectures, and more.

SOME OF MY OTHER BOOKS YOU MAY LOVE

www.sriramananthan.com